D0762969

ADVANCE PRAISE FOR

Extreme Weather Hits Home

Banta's timely advice could help us learn to live with nature with respect and foresight. Too often we trust our city planners, administrators, builders, and other service entities instead of taking personal responsibility for our own health and welfare. Banta provides us with the needed information (tools) to prepare ourselves to face the challenges that global climate change can bring. If knowledge is power, then John Banta has empowered us to live more responsibly and safely.

— Walt Anderson, Professor and Chair of Environmental Studies,
Prescott College. Prescott, Arizona

Banta's book is the Noah's Ark of the twenty-first century. Climb aboard for practical advice, great illustrations and information that will help you preserve and protect your bit of dry earth.

— Jeffrey C. May,
Author of *My House is Killing Me! The Home Guide for Families with Allergies and Asthma*

John Banta takes a complex — and scary — subject and breaks it down into understandable chunks that we can act on. *Extreme Weather Hits Home* empowers us to be less at the mercy of climate change and better able to ride out the storms, even as we work to restore balance to our earth's atmosphere.

— Carol Venolia, architect, coauthor of *Natural Remodeling for the Not-So-Green House*,
and Director of EcoDwelling at New College of California

Banta has done a superb job of addressing the range of potentially devastating impacts upon the residential ecosystem that can result from the spectrum of climate change effects that are anticipated to increase in frequency and severity for some time to come. Blending building and earth sciences in an engrossing narrative style, this book presents the practical and applied knowledge of home protection practices that every current and future homeowner needs to maximize to preserve the building's structure and the health and safety of its occupants, in the face of earth's natural forces.

— Eugene C. Cole, DrPH, Professor of Environmental Health Sciences, Brigham Young University

John Banta's book contains timely, practical, insightful information on a topic of emerging global concern. He clearly explains the key concepts of building science and physics, and their role in how weather-related events can impact the integrity and safety of modern residential dwellings, including indoor environmental quality. This book should be required reading for anybody building or buying a home — as well as builders, architects, engineers, and other residential construction trades and suppliers.

— James Craner, MD, MPH, Occupational and Environmental Medicine

Brilliant ... a very informative book, a must have for property owners. This book will definitely safeguard your home against extreme weather. I look forward to John's next book!

— Joseph J. McDonald, PowerWorks LLC

John Banta's *Extreme Weather Hits Home* is an easy read chocked full of indispensable information for any serious restoration, remediation, construction, insurance or indoor environmental professional. The information and writing style is even clear enough for home or business owners who want to make their buildings more disaster-resistant and to understand restoration basics. John combines a serious collection of environmental and building science with practical solutions based on years of real-life field experience. It doesn't get much better than this!

— Jeff Bishop, Restoration industry author, trainer and
technical advisor Clean Care Seminars, Inc.

As an active member of the Standards Writing Body, John's caring, time and spirit has made an inestimable difference to our industry. He has put the same diligence and passion for the industry into *Extreme Weather Hits Home.*

— Barry D. Costa, Institute of Inspection Cleaning and Restoration,
Certification Standards Chair and President Costa Group, Inc.

Banta has taken the concepts of global warming and rapid climate change, and stretched our understanding to a new level by synthesizing these climatic threats with his thorough knowledge of building dynamics to develop a scientifically sound, yet accessible, publication. This well written and informative volume serves to enlighten and educate, while challenging us to think beyond familiar environmental issues to the immediate environment in which we live our daily lives, and brings global environmental concerns to the doorstep of each of us who share this planet.

— Sean P. Abbott, Ph.D., Microbiologist, Natural Link Mold Lab, Inc.

EXTREME WEATHER
HITS HOME

EXTREME WEATHER HITS HOME

EXTREME WEATHER HITS HOME

Protecting Your Buildings
From Climate Change

JOHN BANTA

NEW SOCIETY PUBLISHERS

Cataloging in Publication Data:
A catalog record for this publication is available from the National Library of Canada.

Cover design by Diane McIntosh. Photos: iStock.

Printed in Canada.
First printing July 2007.

Paperback ISBN: 978-0-86571-593-6

Inquiries regarding requests to reprint all or part of *Extreme Weather Hits Home* should be addressed to New Society Publishers at the address below.

To order directly from the publishers, please call toll-free (North America) 1-800-567-6772, or order online at www.newsociety.com

Any other inquiries can be directed by mail to:

New Society Publishers
P.O. Box 189, Gabriola Island, BC V0R 1X0, Canada
(250) 247-9737

New Society Publishers' mission is to publish books that contribute in fundamental ways to building an ecologically sustainable and just society, and to do so with the least possible impact on the environment, in a manner that models this vision. We are committed to doing this not just through education, but through action. This book is one step toward ending global deforestation and climate change. It is printed on acid-free paper that is 100% post-consumer recycled (**100% old growth forest-free**), processed chlorine free, and printed with vegetable-based, low-VOC inks, with covers produced using Forest Stewardship Council-certified stock. Additionally, New Society purchases carbon offsets based on an annual carbon audit, operating with a carbon-neutral footprint. For further information, or to browse our full list of books and purchase securely, visit our website at: www.newsociety.com

NEW SOCIETY PUBLISHERS   www.newsociety.com

This book is dedicated to my wife Trisha,
my daughters Tiffany and Jamie,
and the generations yet to be born.

Contents

Acknowledgments

I would like to thank the many individuals who provided much help, support and inspiration in writing this book. First, to Jim and Pam Holland: they have provided me a nurturing and creative work environment that has always challenged me to look to the future.

This book was begun due to guidance from Taner Vargonen, and completed with love and support from my personal community of friends: Anne Vargonen, Sheila Foraker, Victor Spiegel, Christine Long, John Rowland, Olwyn Rowland and many others too numerous to mention.

Roy Parks generously shared his time and rescued a major portion of the manuscript for this book from the hard drive when my computer crashed. Misty Parks shared her husband and her wisdom during that stress-filled time. You have both been the best of friends.

Special thanks to architect Helmut Ziehe, friend and founder of the Institute for Baubiology and Ecology in Clearwater, Florida. Helmut's tireless promotion of healthy home environments and translation of the German research in the field of Building Biology have been foundational in helping me understand buildings and what makes them work or fail.

This book couldn't have been written without the help, encouragement and contributions from ecologists, members of the water damage restoration industry, indoor environmental investigators and other professionals. Of special note are Jeff Bishop, Mitchell W. Greer, Bruce Siler, Marion Van Pelt, Bill Spohn, Phil Dawson and J.T. Heater.

My thanks to the specialists who reviewed, commented and assisted with my work: Gilbert Paquette at Lightning Rod Stuff; Jennifer Morgan at East Coast Lightning; Paula Baker LaPorte and Robert LaPorte of EcoNest; Joe Lstiburek of Building Sciences Consulting; David Dybdahl. And my editors: Ingrid Witvoet, Murray Reiss and all the staff at New Society Publishers.

Finally, my gratitude and love to my family. My wife Trish Banta has been by my side for over 30 years. Words can't express my love for her and my appreciation for the sacrifices she has made to help produce this book. And to my daughters Jamie Banta and Tiffany Rice and my son-in-law Charles Lee Rice for their critiques, creativity, time, patience and help in focusing and organizing my manuscript. Each of them added their special talents and support to help write this book.

Foreword

They say that you can tell a man by the company he keeps. John Banta has kept company with some of the greats ... Charley, Francis, Ivan, Wilma and Katrina and has learned first hand what their hurricane force winds and water can do to a home. In fact he has dedicated the last 20 years examining and fixing buildings that have failed to protect against the forces of nature. Some of these have failed as the result of sudden weather events and others have failed slowly and imperceptibly over time until one day their hidden problems became apparent after irreversible damage had already occurred. John is not only a fine restoration consultant; he is a building detective of "Colombo" like stature. He is a keen observer of nature with a specialty in the interface between nature and the man-made world. His wealth of first hand experience and know-how has of late become of great need to all of us and luckily for us John has written it down in *Extreme Weather Hits Home*. John has brought his trove of knowledge to bear in this timely book.

Now with the "quickening" of extreme weather events we must all ask ourselves about the personal impact that global warming will have on us. As inhabitants of a wealthy nation many of us have come to think of tragic loss from natural occurrence as something that happens to someone else, somewhere else. Now, disaster is striking closer to home on a more regular basis and many of us begin to look upon the might of nature with more respect and trepidation and our scientists predict much, much more to come. This is not a book that tells us how to arrest global warming. There is already a wealth of information circulating about how we can all work to reduce our greenhouse emissions to slow down the process of climate change. We all need to become better "citizens of the world" and see the global impact of our individual actions. Simultaneously we need to pay attention to the home front. At best we have already set forces in to motion that will cause change, inconvenience and discomfort and this book tells us how to adapt to these changes and keep our homes and families safer. At worst, if we are not capable as a species of making radical voluntary change, then neither this book nor any other will be of much use.

At this point in time while scientists try to model the effects of global warming two things are apparent: The precise implications of global warming are not now possible to predict on a micro level and more extreme weather events are to be expected. In fact we do not need scientists to tell us that weather conditions are becoming more extreme. One need only listen to the news.

So what are the implications for those of us who are homeowners?

Whenever natural disaster strikes it leaves winners and losers in its wake. John Banta has spent time investigating both. In *Extreme Weather Hits Home* John explains the reasons why homes fail under various climatic circumstances and offers straight-forward, practical and easy-to-follow advice about how to build "insurance" into our homes so that when extreme weather hits home, our homes can withstand or minimize the damage. He shows us how to learn from "other people's" mistakes in the likely event that we will face the unprecedented conditions, receiving "other people's weather". Which other people? Shall we prepare for drought, flood, wind, lightning, fire, record heat or record cold?

If we all had a personal crystal ball then insurance companies would all be out of business. We wouldn't buy car insurance if we could see into the future and know that we would never be in an accident. We would upsize or down-size our home insurance premiums dependant on the future claims we would be making, with certainty. We all pay for insurance policies "just in case". Most of us buy medical insurance *and* practice preventative medicine ... taking vitamins, consuming healthy food, exercising regularly and getting wellness exams. This improves our resiliency and decreases the likelihood of ill-health coming suddenly upon us. Even though our insurance policies may cover the costs of illness we still work hard to avoid ill-health because we don't want to suffer the pain and loss of life quality that are the inevitably bed fellows of illness. John shows us how to practice preventative medicine for our homes. In *Extreme Weather Hits Home* John takes the reader through a thorough yet easy to follow explanation of the many types of extreme weather that we might face and presents solutions. Many of the suggestions throughout the book are simple, easy to implement and provide relatively cheap insurance for our health and safety. John also educates the homeowner about disaster preparedness and what actions to take during an extreme weather event, while waiting for professional help to arrive, so that damage can be minimized for the family and for the home.

The book speaks to the almost certain inevitability of more extreme weather conditions as the results of global warming become apparent. While Insurance companies may pay for damages after-the-fact, foresight and prudent application of strategic measures can protect our homes and the well-being of our families *before* hardship knocks on our door. We can build resiliency and adaptive capacity in to our homes and John Banta shows us how!

This is recommended reading for smart homeowners.

— Paula Baker-Laporte FAIA
www.econest.com

Preface

For the last 20 years I have been investigating buildings that have had problems with indoor environmental issues. I began offering professional environmental consulting services late in 1986. It was about that time when I first learned about the German specialty field of *Baubiologie* or Building Biology. Germany and most of Europe had been greatly ahead of the US in their awareness of indoor air quality problems. Much of that stemmed from the massive amounts of new construction that occurred in European cities after World War II. I learned of Dr. Anton Schneider, one of Germany's leading educators in the field of *Baubiologie*, and wrote to him. He wrote back and informed me that his study materials were being brought to the United States and translated into English by German architect Helmut Ziehe. A short time later my wife and I became acquainted with Helmut. It was through Dr. Schneider's *Baubiologie* course material and Helmut's translation that I came to a more holistic understanding of the mechanisms that were causing problems in buildings. I credit this study with my understanding of how buildings can be built to either work with the environment to establish a safe healthy home for people, or to go against these principles and cause discomfort or ill health for the occupants.

During the last decade the vast majority of the environmental investigative work I have performed has been related to water damage, mold and what goes wrong with buildings. Many of the indoor environmental quality inspections I perform are in problem buildings that turn out to have suffered damage from earthquakes, wind, water, rodents and fire. The past five years have also presented increasing damage from storms and hurricanes. In 2002 I witnessed first hand the power of wind when a tornado turned over a semi-truck trailer in Austin, Texas, a few minutes before I drove by. I have worked on multiple cases of buildings that were damaged in 2004 by hurricanes Charley, Francis and Ivan, as well as Katrina and Wilma in 2005. These years have been some of the most expensive for the insurance industry on record, yet they continue to make record profits. More importantly, the human tragedy and suffering did not end with the disasters.

The uncertainty of what tomorrow will bring means that any changes made to buildings need to make them flexible enough to withstand the potential extremes that may develop on both ends of the climate change pendulum swing. This means we need to be prepared to recognize a variety of conditions that will sometimes shift almost imperceptibly and other times smash into our buildings with literal hurricane force. For existing buildings we need to use our resources to deal with real problems. If we recognize developing problems early, then respond appropriately with first-aid measures, we can limit the damage until more permanent corrections can be made. The climate changes that are becoming apparent are often unpredictable. Just when it appears that a permanent pattern is beginning to emerge the pendulum swings again. The watchword for the future is "flexibility."

In this book I have combined my experience as an environmental consultant and do-it-yourself home remodeler with my studies and observations regarding building failure into a guidebook that anticipates the effects of climate change on our homes and suggests ways we personally can help protect our homes from these changes. I hope this book helps you understand how climate change is resulting in increasing damage to buildings and how you can personally use that knowledge to help secure your property. If society doesn't use our short window of opportunity to get our greenhouse gases under control, we can anticipate that extreme weather patterns will exert stronger and stronger incentives. We have already lost our window of opportunity to do this the easy way and moved into the realm of the hard way. By acting now most people will be able to implement measures to protect their homes with only minor inconveniences. But if we don't implement measures to prevent ever-increasing greenhouse gas emissions, the issues won't be solved by this or any other book.

Introduction

For having lived long, I have experienced many instances of being obliged, by better information or fuller consideration, to change opinions, even on important subjects, which I once thought right but found to be otherwise.

— Benjamin Franklin

Competent authorities agree global warming is occurring and that human activities are causing a rapid acceleration of climate change. Not only is our planet experiencing multiple types of extreme weather events, but their intensity and frequency have also increased. It is also well recognized that climate change is having a direct impact on the natural environment. Coral reefs are bleaching, populations of frogs and many other species are becoming extinct and birds are suffering from limited food supplies where they nest each year. A major contributing factor is the greenhouse gas carbon dioxide, which is rapidly building up in the atmosphere. It has been increasing gradually over the last 100 years after being proven to be relatively stable historically. For your convenience at the back of this book, in the

"Observational evidence from all continents and most oceans shows that many natural systems are being affected by regional climate changes, particularly temperature increases."

(IPCC 2007 page 1 Summary for Policymakers)

1

end notes and essential reading recommendations section, you will find some of the authorities I have quoted as well as many of the resources that I have found to be helpful for learning how to reduce your carbon dioxide impact. This book offers suggestions and advice for protecting our dwellings from the impact of global warming, so that we can prepare for the coming climate changes.

Weather cycles, including extreme weather events, will never completely disappear. Our homes need to be constructed to be more resilient in the face of these cycles. This book starts with the premise that global climate change is occurring and that as the climate shifts, current construction and maintenance practices in various parts of North America will need to readjust in order to prevent structural damage and indoor

Canada's risks from climate change would include increasing intensity of thunderstorm activity resulting in increased wind storms, tornados, lightning, hail and flooding. Melting permafrost already has begun to cause structural damage in northern parts of Canada. As temperatures warm and soil moisture content shifts toward drier conditions the risks from drought and expansive clay soils increase. Presently the recognized areas of expansive clay soils are in some of the more populated central portions of Canada, along the border with the United States. Tornado risks will also increase. Tornados form when cold air from the north meets warmer tropical air from Mexico. As the climate warms it should be anticipated that the frequency of tornados in Canada will increase as the meeting place for the warm and cold air shifts northward. Rising sea levels could also inundate low-lying coastal towns. The risk to buildings from trapped moisture is a potential problem, but chances are the United States will serve as an early warning device since the climate in Canada would need to shift fairly dramatically to go from being a cold climate to a mixed-humid climate. Most Canadians have homes constructed to deal with freezing conditions and frozen plumbing, but problems with ice damming may increase since a warmer climate means the winter temperatures will be closer to the melting point. Typically, when snow remains solidly frozen ice dams don't form. The problems develop when the snow repeatedly defrosts during the day and then refreezes at night so that the water is unable to drain away before it refreezes. The warming trend is likely to increase the incidents of these types of problems in Canada.

air quality problems from developing. This introduction to the damaging conditions that result from climate change, as they may affect our homes and living environments, will serve as a roadmap for prevention measures to help maintain our homes as shifts in climate occur. Some first-aid measures are easy and inexpensive to apply. Other measures may require retrofit techniques for remodeling existing homes to prevent or reduce damage from problems induced by climate change shifts. Modifying our building construction methods to conform to nature's demands will help our homes function properly so that they will not tend to deteriorate and suffer extensive damage.

In order to weather or recover easily from extreme events our homes need to be tuned and maintained to function properly during normal times. If not recognized early, normal wear and tear can provide a weak point for extreme weather or climate change to cause greater and more costly damage. We tune up our cars and change their oil regularly. We visit the doctor for routine checkups. But most people wait for something to break before recognizing problems that are developing in their homes.

North America has a wide variety of climate zones with corresponding construction codes in place. Each of these various zones is based on regional climate differences and generally requires different construction styles for building durability. Buildings certainly can have problems unrelated to climate change. These deficiencies can occur from sloppy construction practices, inadequate maintenance and incorrect remodeling practices which lead to many expensive repairs. As climates change, however, building maintenance and construction practices need to be appropriately adjusted to prevent additional problems. Present construction failures provide clues to

Some part or another of the United States is at risk from every type of extreme weather event discussed in this book. One reason is that the United States includes an incredibly diverse climate and topography spanning multiple climate zones. The lowest and highest points in North America — Death Valley and Mount McKinley — are found in the United States. Alaska sits in the extremely cold north while Florida is located in the hot-humid tropical zone and Hawaii, being surrounded by the Pacific Ocean, exhibits a marine climate.

Most of Mexico is a hot-humid or hot-dry climate. Projections for climate change make it unlikely for Mexico to experience cold climate problems. Temperatures are projected to continue to increase, which is likely to increase risks from wildfire, drought and heat waves. Mexico has few tornados, and most of them occur near the US-Mexico border. Mexican hurricanes are rare. Hurricanes spawn in the Gulf of Mexico but are more likely to make landfall further north. Mexican west coast hurricanes were virtually unheard of until 2006. The risk of expansive clay soils has not been well studied in most of Mexico; however, the condition is well documented in and around Mexico City and Queretaro. Flash flooding is common since rain on dry soils tends to run off instead of seeping into the soil.

what may occur as planetary stresses and climate change begin to affect our homes.

Climate change may result in either acute or chronic problems for our buildings. Most acute problems develop rapidly from extreme weather events where the damage is generally easy to recognize, such as that caused by hurricanes, tornados, flooding events and lightning. These events are often catastrophic for many buildings and sometimes affect entire communities or regions. Chronic weather events such as drought or periods of high humidity, in otherwise moderate climate zones, may result in damage from slower shifts in climates that are less apparent. These damaging climate effects often seem less dramatic, but they can cause as severe or even worse damage than rapid catastrophic events if they aren't discovered and remedied quickly. Fortunately the conditions leading to the chronic effects can often be predicted, or discovered early enough to arrest and reverse the damage. These more slowly developing conditions include structural damage from expansive clay soils in areas experiencing drought or desertification. When expansive clay soils are present in areas where the soil is becoming drier, buildings may slowly be ripped apart, much like an earthquake in slow motion. Expansive clay soils have been recognized as a problem for decades prior to global warming becoming an issue. According to Phil Camp, "The American Society of Civil Engineers estimates that half of the homes in the United States are built on expansive soils and half of these will have some damage. The group claims that these soils are responsible for more home damage every year than floods, tornadoes, and hurricanes combined" (Camp). At this time there have been no studies to determine what percentage of this damage is related to climate change.

Another chronic condition that may result from slow shifts in climate is mold growth and water damage. These don't always require a liquid water spill or flood and may develop from trapped water in a vapor form. Shifts in temperature and humidity can result in water vapor condensing into liquid water in wall cavities. Mold and water damage has sometimes been referred to as "slow fire." Water can cause every bit as much damage to a building as fire, only at a slower rate. Fortunately, most of the problems from water vapor and mold can be prevented if the issues are recognized early and appropriate action is taken.

Most buildings today are constructed in such a way that they will require major remodeling or repairs sometime before they reach the age of 25. Roofs typically need replacement every 15 to 30 years, kitchens and baths are updated as the plumbing and fixtures wear out or become outdated, and most houses need routine painting or sealing. These remodeling events provide an excellent opportunity to begin to respond to climate change by upgrading proactively. A little extra investment in time and money during necessary maintenance activities can prevent or limit costly damages later. By recognizing the climate-related stresses developing in and around your home you may be able to apply temporary measures to control or prevent the deterioration until more permanent remodeling solutions can be instituted.

Extreme Weather Hits Home will not be able to anticipate every condition that may arise from climate change where you live. There are bound to be surprises. It is important to recognize that many of the measures in this book are considered initial steps to protect our homes. However, responding to our planet's changing climate quickly and allowing it to heal itself is, ultimately, the necessary course. Otherwise the widely fluctuating weather patterns and severity of the climate change are likely to worsen to a condition that may be beyond even heroic measures.

As more and more buildings become damaged by extreme weather events, insurance coverage is likely to become more expensive or even unavailable. Many types of damages are already excluded from insurance policies and government disaster assistance programs. Unfortunately, many building owners are unaware of these limitations and are unprepared to deal with them and the financial hardships when they arise.

Professional assistance can help with recovery from many types of losses; however, catastrophic events such as major floods and hurricane damage often result in insufficient community resources being available for a quick and adequate response. Prompt action on the part of the building owner, therefore, can help reduce the adverse impacts. Also, knowing what work needs to be done and when to do it can help the homeowner select and oversee the work force for needed prevention measures or repair.

The preventative measures presented in this book are based on the assumption that we can and will take action that will get carbon dioxide and other greenhouse gas emissions under control. Not all damage resulting from climate change will be avoided, but prompt recognition and application of first-aid techniques may help to reduce the costs of damage, correction and repair to your home. First-aid is used to temporarily sustain a patient's life until more intensive professional help is available. Of course, recognizing the patient is in distress is always the first step that may lead to its successful administration. If it becomes apparent that more drastic action is necessary, temporary first-aid measures can help provide the necessary time for the completion of more extensive retrofit and remodeling measures.

Naturally, if we don't deal with the causes of climate change, this book's first-aid suggestions for your home are likely to provide only short-term or less than adequate results. Long-term unstable climates mean that building codes will need to change and new construction will need to be designed and built to be more resilient. However, if we take definitive action to reduce greenhouse gas emissions, the planet will most likely repair itself and reverse the shifts that are occurring. My goal is to alert you to some of these developing issues and provide suggestions for taking appropriate action, giving you the power to make choices that are best for your family, your home and our planet.

Part One

Climate Change and Your Home: An Overview

One

Why Good Buildings Go Bad

"Perhaps the most valuable result of all education is the ability to make yourself do the thing you have to do when it ought to be done, whether you like it or not; it is the first lesson that ought to be learned; and however early a man's training begins, it is probably the last lesson that he learns thoroughly."

— Thomas Huxley

Building to Last

In order for buildings to withstand problems associated with climate change, they must first be mechanically fit. By that I mean they need to be structurally sound and able to provide for our shelter and protection without being harmed by the elements. Using a body analogy, by German building biology practitioner Dr. Anton Schneider, our homes need strong bones and joints (framing and fasteners). The building's skin (exterior surfaces) needs to be able to keep out the rain snow and wind, while letting perspiration (excess moisture) escape. It needs to have the proper amount of fat (insulation).

North America's timber resources have resulted in most residential structures being built with wood frame construction. The typical home begins with a foundation made of a masonry material that holds up well to water, but once we get above ground level the types of construction materials change so they frequently don't hold up as well to moisture. Wood framing, exterior cladding and interior walls are often made of materials that could make pretty good compost, if they stay wet for a sufficient period of time. It is a given that buildings will get wet, but it is important to remember they will deteriorate rapidly if they *stay* wet. In order to be functional, buildings must shed water and dry reasonably quickly.

I've known building scientist Joe Lstiburek for approximately 15 years. In my opinion, Joe has clarified our understanding of how buildings work and what makes them fail more than any other person in North America. One of the most important things I have learned from Joe is that buildings get wet and it's okay for buildings to get wet as long as they can then dry. I've also learned that some materials can get wet and stay wet longer than other types of material. Living trees are wet wood and can stay wet for hundreds of years. While trees are growing it is common for them to have twice as much water weight as wood weight. The same level of moisture that sustains tree growth will cause the tree to decay once it is dead. Dead spruce, fir and pine wood will begin to rot if 28 percent of their weight is water. Once they start to rot you have to lower the wood moisture content to below 20 percent in order to stop them from rotting and you have to lower the wood moisture content below 16 percent in order to stop mold from growing on their surface. Rotting wood loses its strength slowly, sometimes requiring years to decay.

If we peel wood into layers and glue those layers back together we get plywood. Plywood has more surface area than solid wood, but it is less able to withstand extended elevated levels of moisture; however, it still does a pretty good job. If we flake the solid wood and then glue the wood chips back together under pressure with waxes and resins we get oriented strand board (OSB). Oriented strand board has more wood surface area in the chips than plywood has with the peeled wood sheets, so the OSB doesn't hold up as well to moisture as plywood. It can get wet, but if it stays wet long enough for the moisture to penetrate through the board, it will swell and start to fall apart in a matter of weeks. If we grind the wood into sawdust and glue it back together we get particle board. Particle board has more wood surface area in the particles than OSB has in the chips, so the particle board doesn't hold up as well to moisture as the OSB. Particle board can get wet, but if it stays wet long enough for the moisture to penetrate through the board, it will swell and start to fall apart in a matter of a few days. If we cook and process the wood particles, they separate into cellulose fibers which are used to make paper. Paper has a tremendous amount of processed, tenderized and blended wood cellulose fibers. When paper gets wet it begins to fall apart and decay quickly. It is a perfect predigested food for mold. The "Three Little Pigs" provide a lesson that continues to hold true. Straw and sticks don't have the longevity of brick, stone and other types of masonry materials.

According to Joe, "Even the dumbest of the three little pigs didn't build their homes out of paper." Yet almost every modern building in North America has the interior wrapped with paper, with one of the most prevalent types being the paper found on gypsum wallboard. The gypsum center absorbs and holds the water like a sponge in direct contact with the paper it is faced with. Basically, we are building our homes with instant mold food — just add water, let it sit for a few days, and dinner is served. With a little water for a long time (weeks to months), or a lot of water for a little time (days), we get mold on gypsum wallboard paper, paper underlayment and latex carpet binder, but the solid wood is generally fine. If there is a problem on the wood, it develops first on the surface and where the wood was in contact with the paper.

To develop strategies for preventing or limiting damage to buildings from climate change it is necessary to understand properly functioning buildings. A primary purpose of our homes is to provide us shelter. When it is cold outside, our homes should keep us warm. When it is hot outside, they should keep us cool. Homes should shield us from events such as wind, rain, snow, hail and solar radiation. All of these tasks have been performed by buildings to one degree or another through the centuries.

Traditionally, successful homes were constructed based on an understanding of annual cycles and rhythms. "Master builders" were craftsmen with an understanding of every step of the construction process from the foundation to the finish work. Homes were built above flood levels. Either the land was high enough with good drainage to prevent flooding, or structures were put on stilts or piers. In cold areas, homes needed to trap heat. In warm areas they needed to take advantage of natural cooling breezes, evaporative cooling or be sheltered from the sun. Over time these master builders learned the types of construction that would be durable and withstand the elements.

Home builders used to construct buildings that would last for a long time. For example, when I visited England to teach a class about mold remediation I was able to take some time to tour northern England. During the trip it quickly became apparent that craftsmen in England knew how to build for longevity. One town, named Kirkwhelpington, stands just a short distance from the Scottish border. It is a small village made up of stone masonry structures. The oldest buildings in town were the church and the vicarage, which were probably completed in the early 1200s. Today both buildings are fully functional and will probably be around long after most of the buildings that are currently built in North America have turned to rubble. Most of the town was made up of buildings that were over a century old. These buildings had a character and age that deserved veneration. Repeatedly, I heard owners express with pride the attitude that when they moved into one of these historical buildings they were gladly accepting the role of a short-term caretaker and guardian for a building that would be around much longer than the people that inhabited them.

These buildings aren't free of problems; they just have different types of problems than found in most of the buildings in North America. Some of the masonry buildings I observed during this trip were dank with moisture, but the structure of the walls and foundation were still holding up well. It became apparent that the skills and methods that were needed for many restoration projects in England were very different, because oddly enough the types of construction were very durable. Obviously a dank, wet masonry building isn't the best for occupants, or their furnishings and possessions, even if the building can last for thousands of years. However most of the older buildings I observed had been remodeled to be quite comfortable, warm and inviting.

Modern construction using products like particle board, oriented strand board, and other composite materials tends to be less forgiving and more likely to begin to fall apart if not properly maintained.

In the 1970s, when the energy crisis hit North America, construction practices began

All components of a building must drain water away from the interior to prevent moisture accumulation and building deterioration. A drainage plane in a wall system creates an easy pathway for water to drain away from the house.

Construction on this stone masonry church in Kirkwelpington, England, was completed in the early 1200s. The building is still in use and in excellent condition.

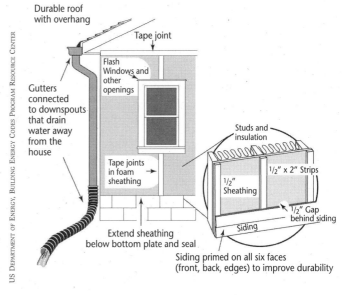

US Department of Energy, Building Energy Codes Program Resource Center

Durable roof with overhang

Tape joint

Flash Windows and other openings

Gutters connected to downspouts that drain water away from the house

Tape joints in foam sheathing

Extend sheathing below bottom plate and seal

Studs and insulation

1/2" x 2" Strips

1/2" Sheathing

1/2" Gap behind siding

Siding

Siding primed on all six faces (front, back, edges) to improve durability

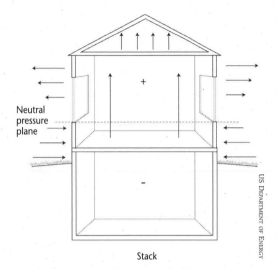

Neutral pressure plane

Stack

US DEPARTMENT OF ENERGY

Stack effect is caused by warm air rising. In some older buildings, cool air pulled from under the building acts as natural air conditioning. In newer homes it is more likely to trap moisture along with radon or other harmful gases that are pulled from the soil.

to change quite dramatically to make buildings more energy efficient. Buildings were insulated, tightened and sealed to reduce energy consumption while keeping their temperature comfortable. As buildings became tighter they tended to retain more moisture. During the summer months this indoor moisture could be removed by the dehumidification provided by a properly operating air conditioning system. Unfortunately, depending on the materials and construction methods used, the moisture might stay trapped in the wall cavities and condense on cold surfaces on the inside of the wall, much the same as moisture droplets form on the outside of a glass of ice water. Some of the first mold problems resulting as a consequence of energy conservation measures began to develop from trapped moisture in buildings, but it took about a decade for the number of well-insulated, moisture-trapping buildings to increase to the point where these problems began to be recognized.

We want to keep our homes dry to prevent them from falling apart, but how dry do they need to be? Our homes have a certain capacity to withstand moisture. Joe Lstiburek has done the math and tells us that a 2,000-square-foot solid masonry structure, like the ones I observed during my trip to England have a capacity, when dry, to absorb up to about 500 gallons of excess water vapor from the air before reaching a moisture capacity that would allow surface molds to grow on sensitive paper-containing materials like gypsum wallboard and various types of underlayment. The same size structure built with wood framing, when dry, could absorb about 50 gallons of excess water vapor before reaching a level that would permit mold growth. Finally our metal-framed homes have very little excess water capacity and can only tolerate about five gallons of excess water vapor.

Big heavy masonry buildings absorb the excess water vapor when conditions are wet and release it back into the building when conditions are dry. This is an ideal cycle and helps to maintain a healthy ☛

Homes that are being built today are for the most part mechanically controlled sealed boxes. They can handle a certain amount of moisture, but their moisture handling capabilities are easily exceeded. Buildings with newer construction have also become less forgiving of mistakes in

interior level of moisture. Because they can hold so much excess water, at least temporarily, keeping it unavailable for decay-causing organisms, masonry structures can be extremely forgiving of moisture problems. Wood frame structures are about ten times less forgiving of temporary excess moisture than masonry, but they are much more affordable, and in North America have performed reasonably well as long as the building was constructed using real wood and not built as a tight, energy efficient structure surrounded in paper. The energy crisis changed that. Buildings had to be energy efficient or they ceased to be comfortable. We couldn't afford the excess utility bills. We can no longer afford to be at the mercy of foreign oil, and we can't afford to continue the excessive use of fuels that promote global warming. This means that buildings must be energy efficient *and* they must be designed to deal with the water vapor that is a part of our living environment if we expect them to last.

An average adult exhales about a quart of water every day. Bathing, cooking, washing clothes and dishes can contribute another gallon or more. A normal concrete slab in a 2,000-square-foot home will release up to half a gallon of water vapor each day.

If more moisture accumulates each day than is removed from the building the moisture begins to accumulate inside the building until the materials can no longer safely hold any more and deterioration begins. If a typical family releases two and a half more gallons of water vapor into the building each day than is being removed by ventilation and air conditioning, the family living in a masonry house that started out dry would have 200 days to get their moisture under control before materials became wet enough to begin to decay. A wood frame house would provide about twenty days to get it together and metal framing a mere two days of moisture buffering capacity. Modern buildings don't have the capacity to hold as much water because the materials we build with are less forgiving. In addition our buildings are tighter which tends to retain more moisture inside.

The recommendations for construction techniques that should be used for your current climate zone are available from Joe Lstiburek's website at buildingscience.com. He has posted a huge number of articles and publications that detail how buildings should function for your particular zone.

the types of materials and installation methods. Older buildings would get wet and dry out. Moisture problems were unusual. Today when buildings get wet the moisture tends to be locked in and they do not dry out by themselves as easily. It's like putting a wet towel in a plastic bag. Once moisture gets trapped in modern buildings it can't easily escape.

Modern Materials

It would be great if the design and construction of our homes placed a greater emphasis on techniques and materials necessary for long-lasting buildings but such construction is costly. When many of the less expensive modern construction materials get wet, they tend to stay wet. This means they don't last as long. Gypsum wallboard with paper facing is less forgiving than traditional lath and plaster. Oddly enough, the paper on the gypsum board provides an almost ideal nutrient source for mold growth. The gypsum material in the center can only hold about one percent of its total weight in moisture before it becomes saturated. Some molds can start to grow when the amount of water present is even less than 0.7 percent (ACGIH). Wood lath can handle about 20 times more moisture than the paper on gypsum board before it reaches a point where it supports mold growth. Plaster won't grow mold regardless of how wet it gets, although it can hold moisture and transfer that moisture to other surfaces or paints that are applied to the plaster surface, which in turn may support mold growth.

A challenge for modern construction has been to create a building that maintains a moisture balance using materials and construction practices that are affordable and energy efficient. A typical affordable wall construction in a northern climate from the outside to the inside wall would be made of painted exterior siding, asphalt-impregnated felt, sheathing, wood framing, insulation, a vapor barrier, gypsum wallboard with paper and flat paint. The vapor barrier frequently comes attached to the insulation and is usually installed by stapling the vapor barrier to the interior side of the wood framing, which is the warm side of the wall. This layering of materials and the order of installation has a very important role to play in a home's basic ability to defend itself against moisture and mold growth.

Moisture Flow and Vapor Barriers

It is commonly thought that roofs, walls and foundations are built to be watertight. This is rarely the case. Most roofs, walls and foundations are built to keep most water out, but small amounts will enter that must be directed or drained back out of the building. Residual water that is unable to drain needs to leave the building by evaporation. The longer a building stays wet the greater the risk of deterioration. When a building is functioning properly, most of the water striking the exterior will drain away and the rest will evaporate before it can cause a problem. Protective coatings are frequently added to keep water out, and they do help reduce the amount of moisture sucked up by porous exterior materials. The problem is that some of these same protective coatings, such as elastomeric paint, may impede the building's ability to drain or dry the moisture that does get trapped behind them.

Temperature differences between the indoor and outdoors have an important influence on the direction in which water vapor travels through porous materials. Water vapor tends to move from warmer temperatures to colder. The southernmost parts of the United States tend to be warmer outside than inside most days of the year. Even in the coldest month of January, homes built in Miami, Florida, will typically be exposed to a daily high temperature of 70°F. This means that water vapor in these southern states is predominately trying to move towards the interior of homes where it is cooler from air conditioning. Once the water vapor reaches the interior of the building, it needs to be removed to prevent moisture accumulation.

Vapor retarders are typically installed on the "warm-in-winter" side of the insulation.

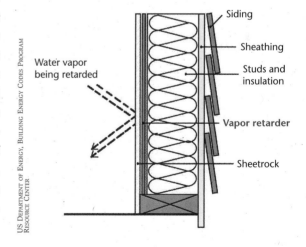

US DEPARTMENT OF ENERGY, BUILDING ENERGY CODES PROGRAM RESOURCE CENTER

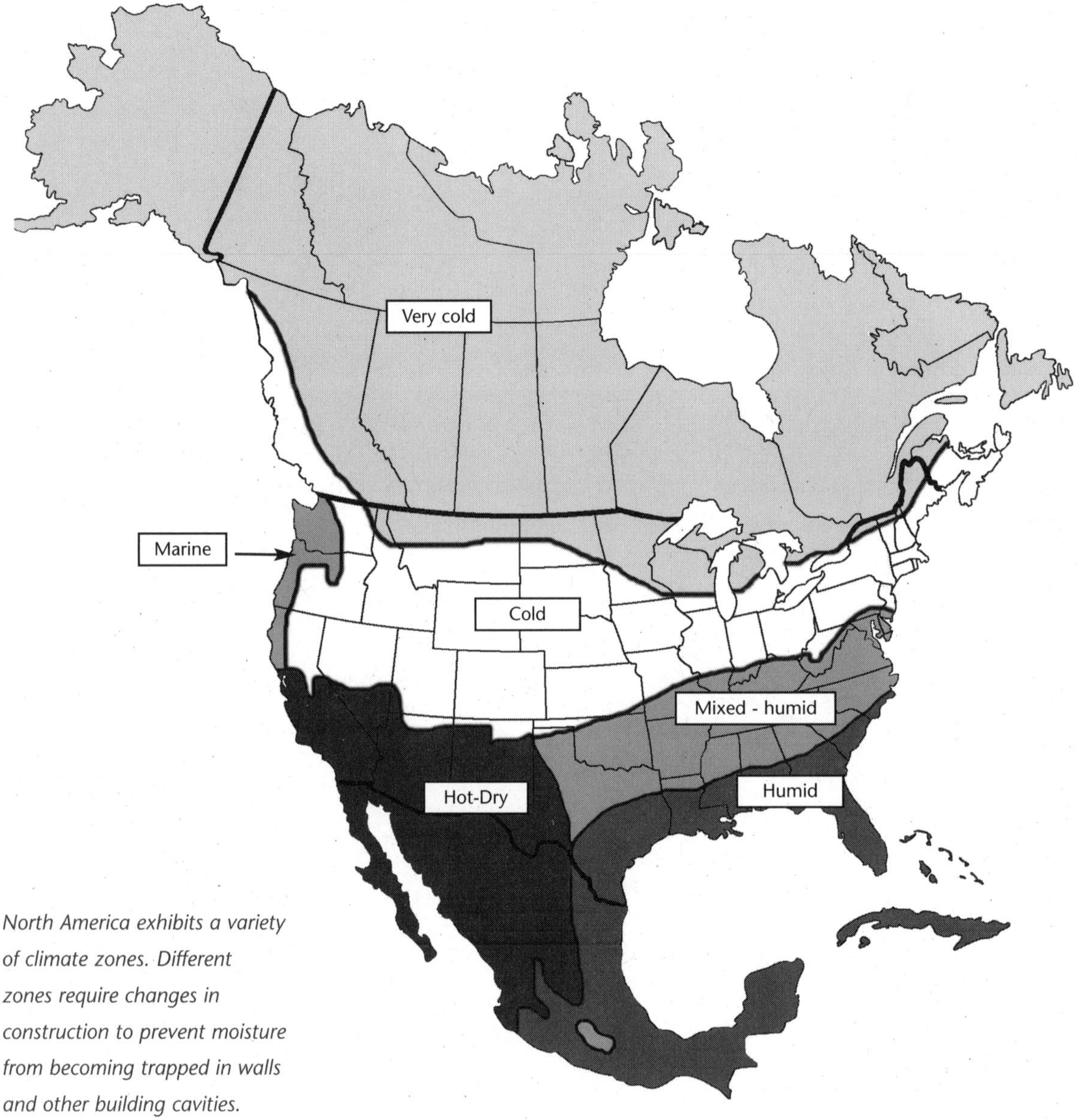

Marine

Very cold

Cold

Marine

Mixed - humid

Hot-Dry

Humid

North America exhibits a variety of climate zones. Different zones require changes in construction to prevent moisture from becoming trapped in walls and other building cavities.

ADAPTED FROM US DEPARTMENT OF ENERGY, BUILDING ENERGY CODES PROGRAM RESOURCE CENTER

The escape of moisture through the wall assemblies of homes in Canada and Alaska is typically in the opposite direction of the moisture flow in southern states. Northern parts of the country typically don't require air conditioning since the average outside temperature is rarely above 70°F. Since moisture moves from warm to cold, these northern homes will typically have the moisture flow from the interior going toward the outside for all but brief periods when high outdoor temperatures cause the flow to reverse. In southern states like Florida the moisture flows from the outside into the home for all but brief periods when it reverses.

So far I've been talking about conditions in cold northern areas and hot-humid southern areas, but much of North America has broader weather extremes where winters become very cold and summers become very hot. These parts of the country with mixed-climate zones present challenging and difficult problems when vapor barriers are being installed. Take for example a mixed-humid climate such as is present in most of the state of Tennessee. The summer months are hot and humid, but in winter the weather becomes much colder and temperatures can plunge to freezing. This means that moisture is traveling from the outside to the inside of buildings during summer and from the inside to the outside in winter. If a vapor barrier is present inside a wall in a mixed-climate zone there is a good chance that it will be on the wrong side of the wall and trap moisture for a portion of each year.

During the summer when air conditioning is being used in these mixed-climates, the water vapor tends to flow toward the colder air-conditioned interior. During this time of the year the vapor barrier would need to be installed toward the warmer outside of the building. During the cold winter months the flow of water vapor reverses and is generally flowing toward the outside, so the vapor barriers would need to be placed towards the warmer interior. This obviously won't work, because the barrier would need to be moved every six months. If the vapor barrier is vinyl wallpaper on gypsum wallboard with paper facing, mold growth is likely to occur under the vinyl wall covering on the gypsum paper during the air-conditioned part of the year. Vapor barriers shouldn't be used at all in mixed-climate conditions where the inside is warmer than the outside for part of the year and colder for the other parts. Vapor-retarding membranes that function as air barriers should be considered instead. However, they may or may not be appropriate depending on the conditions that may occur. Each situation needs to be considered individually based on the anticipated climate. The wider the temperature swings in the outdoor environment as compared to the indoor environment, the greater the risk from moisture accumulation. This primarily applies to the humid middle part of the United States east of the Rocky Mountains. Unfortunately, many homes in these parts of the United States have had vapor barriers installed during construction. In some areas of North America the building code has caused problems by requiring the installation of vapor barriers to help with energy conservation. This was a short-sighted requirement that probably did help conserve energy use, but has had the unfortunate side effect of trapping moisture during a portion of each year.

Some builders have reasoned that the walls should have a vapor barrier placed on both sides of the wall. In theory this should work well, but in practice this usually leads to major problems. The problem is that water vapor travels very well on the unintended air currents that are often present in walls. Every hole in the wall, such as an electrical power outlet or a crack along the baseboard, creates a potential entry point for water vapor to pass through and into the wall cavities. Once inside the wall it may get trapped and begin to accumulate. At first the wood framing can absorb some of the excess moisture. When the moisture levels become high enough the wood's absorptive capacity is saturated and the water vapor will begin to condense as a liquid. This condensation occurs where the water vapor contacts the coldest surface. The liquid water becomes trapped in the wall cavity between the two vapor barriers and can't escape back out of the wall cavity in either direction.

The middle and southern parts of the United States west of the Rocky Mountains tend to have drier outdoor climates and have been less sensitive to problems caused by temperature differences between the interior and the exterior at different times of the year. If climate change results in higher outdoor humidity levels moisture migration could begin to cause climate change related problems with trapped moisture. However, this is considered unlikely. These areas can still experience problems when an interior vapor barrier traps moisture in the walls from landscaping or irrigation water coming in contact with the building. During the summer months the tendency would be for moisture to flow from the warmer outside of the home toward the air-conditioned inside. If moisture from watering plants or from other sources gets the outside of the building repeatedly wet, the moisture may flow into the wall and be blocked from escaping until temperature conditions reverse to allow drying. This repeated wetting of the exterior of the building could also be a problem when interior vapor barriers have been installed in desert regions that have a monsoon season. This is especially true for walls that have sunlight heating them during or immediately after these short but heavy rains that occur in the Southwest during the summer monsoon season.

Maintenance, Upkeep and Remodeling

Even if a building is properly designed and constructed, materials can deteriorate from age and improper maintenance. Homeowners must be vigilant. Gutters and drains that clog need to be routinely cleaned. Any time the building has repairs or remodeling, various components may end up being installed improperly, resulting in the same types of problems as when new construction isn't performed correctly. Another problem is when one trade causes damage to another trade's work.

It is also the responsibility of homeowners to maintain protective and aesthetic coatings, but improper product use is frequently an issue. For example water vapor needs to be able to escape. Elastomeric coatings may be great for use on the outside of a building in the deep South where humidity is trying to move into the building through the walls year-round. On the other hand, vinyl wallpaper can cause disasters when it is installed in these same parts of the country. Depending on the location and conditions, each of these products may cause problems by blocking the flow of moisture and preventing the building from drying properly.

With more homeowners attempting weekend remodeling projects, it is becoming more common to observe remodeling errors that push our buildings closer to having moisture problems.

A homeowner who is in tune with his or her building and the way it works will be better able to recognize signs of the building no longer working and to carefully evaluate and determine what repairs are necessary. If a building is properly constructed for a particular part of the country and the damage is from something like rodents chewing through walls and building nests in the insulation, then the repair should return the building back to the construction that was present before the damage. If on the other hand the damage has been caused by an inappropriate construction technique, or a shift in climate, then repairing the building the same way it was originally built will end up with the damage reoccurring.

The problems that presently occur in some buildings allow us to extrapolate the conditions that will cause millions of existing buildings to have problems in the future due to climate changes.

Two

How Homes are Damaged by Climate Change

A scientific truth does not triumph by convincing its opponents and making them see the light, but rather because its opponents eventually die and a new generation grows up that is familiar with it.

— Max Planck

Climate change is not resulting in a steady, even warming of the planet. The changes are occurring gradually, but with a great deal of pendulum-like extremes. Although the climate in general is warming, the weather is demonstrating greater variability.

It doesn't take special scientific studies to see that unusual weather events are becoming more common. Over the last several years almost everyone has observed some of the effects that extreme weather conditions have on buildings. It was recognized prior to hurricane Katrina that the Louisiana and Mississippi coasts were at risk from hurricanes. Add to that the aging levee system that kept water from engulfing the low-lying areas and the risks multiplied. Buildings in low-lying areas that rely on mechanical interventions need a great deal of ongoing protective effort. Power fails, pumps burn out, land erodes,

"Over the course of this century, net carbon uptake by terrestrial ecosystems is likely to peak before mid-century and then weaken or even reverse, thus amplifying climate change."

(IPCC 2007 page 6 Summary for Policymakers)

"A global assessment of data since 1970 has shown it is likely that anthropogenic warming has had a discernible influence on many physical and biological systems."

(IPCC 2007 page 2
Summary for Policymakers)

muskrats dig holes. Any one of these would be a minor problem that could be easily fixed if it happened alone. But when extreme weather conditions affect an area it is common for multiple problems to develop simultaneously and the typical stress relievers to be exceeded. Stress from climate change is a factor that has not been engineered into most of our residential structures or communities. Steady predictable change is easy to plan for. Unpredictable changes are much more difficult because what is effective in preventing problems from developing in buildings today may become the cause of a problem later. The best strategy to prevent or limit climate change and extreme weather events from harming our homes is to understand the types of possibly temporary shifts in environmental conditions that may occur and develop a variety of methods for responding to them, rather than implementing permanent changes by major remodeling. Extreme weather isn't always violent; it may also be subtle, so that many of our responses can be measured and planned.

We are just beginning to understand some of the planet's very intricate ways of maintaining its balance. This means it is sometimes difficult to accurately predict what exactly will happen with the weather. For this reason if higher-cost remodeling measures are taken, they should be designed to provide the building greater flexibility or resilience to a wide range of conditions instead of protection for only one kind of extreme weather event. Our planning shouldn't be limited to preparation for more frequent heat waves and increases in temperature. We should also be able to deal with the potential for the occasional cold snap as well.

We can get some clues about what to expect from historical weather events. The planet intermittently produces its own greenhouse gas emissions from volcanic vents and other events, but these levels are generally short-term and relatively moderate. Really extreme events in the past have been followed by massive extinctions. If we don't get our artificially created emissions under control we can expect the resulting swings will continue to become more and more extreme. At some point the swings may reach a tipping point that renders portions of the planet uninhabitable. In one doomsday scenario the freshwater polar ice melts and dilutes the deep saltwater Atlantic currents so that the warm tropical waters are no longer transported northwards and a new ice age begins. As the ice at the poles reforms the salinity is reestablished and the cycle is repaired. Of course the "temporary" extreme conditions that result could render those parts of the planet uninhabitable for quite a while.

"Adaptation to climate change is likely to benefit from experience gained in reaction to extreme climate events, by specifically implementing proactive climate change risk management adaptation plans."

(IPCC 2007 page 10
Summary for Policymakers)

It is undoubtedly true that some aspects of global warming will provide certain sectors of the population with advantages. It is likely that some areas of North America will benefit from reduced energy use in the winter, increased crop productions on northern lands, or from ships using a northern passage between the Atlantic and Pacific Oceans instead of the Panama Canal. These positive effects are unlikely to outweigh the overwhelming adverse ramifications. According to research published by the Pew Center, "Climate change resulting from increased greenhouse gas concentrations has the potential to harm societies and ecosystems. ... Reductions in emissions of greenhouse gases and their concentration in the atmosphere will tend to reduce the degree and likelihood that significantly adverse conditions will result." They continue: "... recognition is increasing that the combination of continued increases in emissions and the inertia of the climate system means that some degree of climate change is inevitable. Even if extreme measures could be instantly taken to curtail global emissions, the momentum of the earth's climate is such that warming cannot be completely avoided" (Easterling).

The measures suggested in this book will not prevent buildings from being destroyed by extreme events. They may help lessen the damage, or temporarily increase their durability. But if we don't get our greenhouse gases under control the shifts may become so extreme and unpredictable, and increase so rapidly it won't matter how much our buildings are modified. The National Aeronautic Space Administration's climate scientist James Hansen has stated: "I think we have a very brief window of opportunity to deal with climate change ... no longer than a decade at the most" (Hansen). If he is correct, and there are significant signs pointing in that direction, we need to get busy or all the first-aid measures won't be sufficient to save our buildings or our lifestyle.

One of the most confusing aspects of climate change is that the changes don't occur in the same way everywhere, but swing back and forth between greater and greater extremes. An explanation of some of the conditions that result from extreme weather events will help understand the measures necessary to protect our homes.

Extreme Weather

It is very clear that some types of weather events are extreme. Tornados, hurricanes and lightning storms are all very impressive. However, extreme weather doesn't always mean violent or catastrophic events will occur. These catastrophic events are certainly an important consideration, but a lot of the damage caused by weather is slow and may not be recognized immediately. With this in mind we must consider that gradual changes in weather conditions may have extreme results.

Global Temperature: Land-Ocean Index

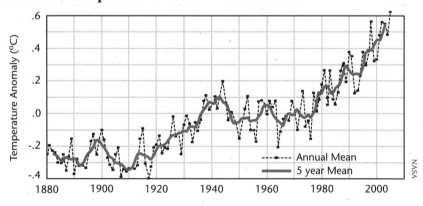

A global rise in temperature has been observed over the last century.

First Effect of Warming Temperatures: Greater Concentration of Moisture

Warmer temperatures allow the mixture of gases in our atmosphere to contain a higher concentration of water vapor. At 70°F the air can mix with only about half as much total moisture as when the temperature is 90°F. When a mass of 90°F air hits a cold weather front it will give up approximately twice as much water in the form of rain as if that same cold front encountered a 70°F mass of air. Higher temperatures mean more potential water vapor and energy that can be released to cause damage to our homes.

"By mid-century, annual average river runoff and water availability are projected to increase by 10-40% at high latitudes and in some wet tropical areas, and decrease by 10-30% over some dry regions at mid-latitudes and in the dry tropics, some of which are presently water stressed areas."

(IPCC 2007 page 5 Summary for Policymakers)

Second Effect of Warming Temperatures: Great Potential for Condensation

The relationship between temperature and humidity creates a greater risk for damage from long-term condensation. Everyone has experienced a cold object developing a film of moisture on its surface. The warm moist air condenses on the colder material. This is true whether we are talking about cold window glass or a can of soda just out of the refrigerator. A rule of thumb is that under normal temperature conditions, like we typically experience in our homes, a 20 degree drop in temperature will result in a doubling of the relative humidity. Relative humidity is expressed as a percentage. When we reach 100 percent relative humidity the air can't hold any further moisture and condensation of the excess moisture occurs.

A number of years ago I had a client who was moving from Australia to the United States. She had decided to bring her furniture with her by shipping it. Many of the items had been hand-made by members of an Aboriginal tribe. Sydney, Australia during the summer can be hot and humid. Let's assume the temperature was 97°F and the humidity was 50 percent (it was probably higher) when her furniture was loaded into the cargo container. The container was then sealed so that it was relatively airtight and transported to the coast where it was loaded into the cargo

Changes in mean annual precipitation from 1975 to 1995 compared to simulations of the projected period 2040 to 2060 are shown here. On average, precipitation increases throughout Canada and the western United States and decreases in the south-eastern United States and much of Mexico.

compartment of a freighter. We will never know exactly what happened but the temperature in the hold of a ship is typically moderate since the hold is below water. For the sake of discussion let's say it was 57°F. If the moisture in the air is sealed into the cargo container along with the household items, then the total amount of water molecules present wouldn't change during the shipment. The relative humidity inside the sealed container will change depending on the temperature. If we lower the temperature from 97°F to 77°F the relative humidity in the container would double and reach the dew point so that condensation begins to form. In the case of my client there was a 40°F difference between the original temperature and the shipping temperature. The excess water vapor becomes liquid water. If the amount of water present is greater than can be absorbed by the furniture and contents in the container, the extra moisture is available to support mold growth on the surface of the items.

During the trip from Australia to California it probably "rained" inside the sealed cargo container for most of the trip. The water condensed on my client's furniture, keeping it wet. By the time her belongings were unloaded mold had grown on practically every surface. In this case my client had the foresight to purchase mold insurance for her shipment, so the damage ended up being paid for, but she would much rather have had her furniture undamaged. The same mechanism that caused the condensation on the furniture can also cause condensation to form inside wall cavities when there are significant differences in temperature between the inside and the outside of the building.

In Chapter One, we explored some of the factors that cause homes to work properly. If buildings aren't designed, built and maintained to protect them from damage, problems can develop that trap moisture in walls and other building spaces. This may lead to mold, rot and other forms of degradation. I also discussed the importance of constructing buildings in ways that are appropriate for their climate. Climate change,

"Based on climate model results, it is very unlikely that the Meridional Overturning Circulation (MOC) in the North Atlantic will undergo a large abrupt transition during the 21st century. Slowing of the MOC this century is very likely, but temperatures over the Atlantic and Europe are projected to increase nevertheless, due to global warming."

(IPCC 2007 page 15 Summary for Policymakers)

however, is causing climates to shift. Imagine placing your home that was built for a northern climate on wheels and rolling it south to a new climate zone. If this climate zone requires different construction materials or techniques than those used for your home, problems are likely to develop. One of these is moisture accumulation in wall cavities or other hidden spaces. As climates shift more buildings will accumulate moisture. When this happens cold temperatures on the outside of the walls are likely to cause it to rain inside the walls.

Third Effect of Warming Temperatures: Greater Intensity

As average temperatures increase, the amount of rain is also increasing throughout much of North America. These rains are more extreme, with more rain falling in shorter periods of time. Greater quantities of wind and rain are placing even more stress and causing greater damage to homes exposed to these extreme conditions.

Storms are also more intense. One reason is that warmer temperatures mean more water vapor is present and mixed with the rest of the gases that make up our atmosphere. The amount of energy in the water

When temperature falls, humidity rises. At 50 percent relative humidity a 20-degree drop in temperature results in condensation.

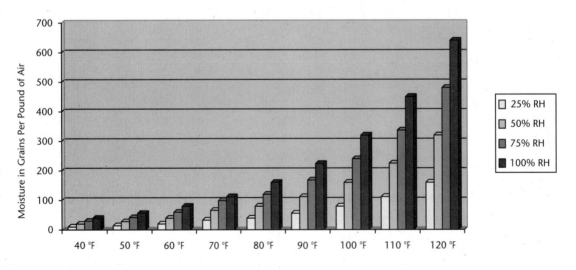

vapor in the air is also greater. The conditions that cause rain to fall typically involve temperature differences between large masses of air. Higher temperatures result in more energy in the atmosphere causing thunderstorms to form. When thunderstorm activity results in tornados, larger temperature differences between hot and cold air masses tend to result in a greater intensity of a storm. Greater intensity usually means more damage to structures that are in the way. Compared to hurricanes, tornados are generally smaller and intensely concentrated swirling winds occurring over land, with an average diameter of 500 feet.

Hurricanes are also swirling masses of air, but originate over water. In order for a hurricane to form the minimum water temperature needs to be around 80°F. The higher the water temperature the greater the hurricane's energy and the faster its wind speeds. Generally, as hurricanes encounter land masses they lose intensity, but they can regain intensity when they pass back out over warm water. The warm water provides a greater amount of energy than found on land, resulting in hurricanes that can be hundreds of miles across. Observation of the images from the damages caused by the extreme wind and water from the 2004 and 2005 hurricane seasons shows the amount of devastation that can occur.

"Since the IPCC Third Assessment, confidence has increased that some weather events and extremes will become more frequent, more widespread and/or more intense during the 21st century; and more is known about the potential effects of such changes."

(IPCC 2007 page 14
Summary for Policymakers)

Fourth Effect From Warming Temperatures: Drier Soil

Warmer temperatures create drier soil conditions. Earlier I pointed out that the warming trend is resulting in greater quantities of rain. What is counterintuitive or seems contradictory, is that more rain doesn't mean more moisture will be accumulated or absorbed by the soil. Intense rains tend to provide too much water too quickly for it to soak into dry soils. The excess water is lost as runoff and flash flooding. Once the soil has dried, it is more difficult to get the moisture back into the soil. A few inches of rain spread over a week will add much more moisture to the soil than if that same amount fell in a few hours. With warmer temperatures leading to increased evaporation and more intense rain running off instead of recharging the soil, the shift in soil moisture is leading to desertification or a drying effect in the soils in many parts of the US. Loss of soil moisture can also cause major shifting in buildings constructed on expansive clay soils. These soils are called expansive because they swell when they absorb water. They also shrink back to a smaller volume as they dry. It is unlikely that all the expansive soil under a building will move in exactly the same way. The different movements of the soil will move the home in different directions causing extensive damage. As climate change causes soils to become drier we can expect the number of buildings damaged by the expansion and contraction of these clay soils to increase.

The drying effects from warmer atmospheric temperatures are also creating a greater risk of fire. The 2006 fire season started early and ended late. The 2007 fire season has also begun early. Recent fire losses have become much greater. There has been speculation that many of these larger fires occur because of a greater amount of underbrush and accumulated fuel. This certainly can be a factor, but a reduction in soil moisture also increases the risk of a more intense fire.

A New Ice Age?

A new reality of global warming is emerging. The warming trends are not resulting in a gentle rise in temperature that will allow adaptation to occur. Instead we are experiencing conditions that are more damaging and difficult to accurately predict. While some weather trends are now being predicted with a fair degree of accuracy, specific events usually can't be anticipated by long-term predictions. The US Global Change Research Program is sufficiently concerned with the possibility of abrupt climate change to have sponsored research by the National Academy of Sciences. Their report identifies many possible scenarios that may develop and areas where significant additional research is needed.

According to the Hadley Centre (the official climate change research center for the United Kingdom) there is a less than five percent chance that the Atlantic Gulf Stream could collapse resulting in another ice age. Should this occur, it is unlikely that we would be able to survive well in affected areas. The extreme cold would freeze the soil under our buildings resulting in shifting and heaving from the expansion of the frozen water in the soil. Pipes would freeze and burst, but these would be minor concerns when we consider that buildings would be buried under tons of snow and ice.

Lesser Extreme Cold Weather Events

Even without another ice age, we still need to be prepared for extreme weather events involving ice

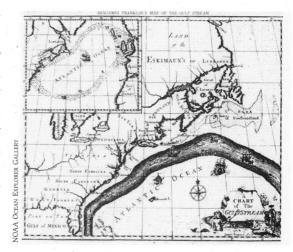

An early sketch of the Gulf Stream by Ben Franklin. The Gulf Stream plays an important role in maintaining the balance that prevents a new Ice Age.

In his book *Water in Buildings,* Architect William Rose tells us that according to the insurance industry the greatest losses from freezing weather conditions don't occur in parts of the country that commonly freeze. "The claims come much more from the southern United States than from the northern states. Texas and Florida were highest on a per capita basis; Minnesota was the lowest. We can attribute this to the surprise factor — Minnesotans build such that freezing pipes are unlikely, whereas southerners may be caught by surprise by an unexpected cold wave. ... Insurance companies paid around $4.5 billion in the 10-year period 1985-1995 in claims for pipes bursting" (Rose). Frozen pipes, ice dams, heaving foundations and overloaded roofs are all rare conditions in the north where people are prepared for them, but become epidemic when very cold weather hits the southern parts of North America. Plumbing installed in southern states is rarely insulated and frequently has some point where it comes above ground such as water shut-off valves and entry points into the building. Furthermore it's common for buildings in the same general vicinity to be constructed similarly so when failures occur they tend to be repeated at the neighbors' homes as well.

and snow. Although temperatures are warming at the planet's surface and in the troposphere, further research at Los Alamos National Laboratory has demonstrated the stratosphere has cooled substantially (Keller). This has resulted in an extreme difference between the temperatures of the near and outer atmospheres. This temperature difference is one of the forces driving more extreme weather events. It is clear that even with a warming of the climate, cold snaps are going to occur.

The greatest damage from unusual cold conditions occurs in areas that do not frequently experience unusual cold. A couple of years ago in Atlanta, Georgia, an unusual weather condition temporarily shut down the airport due to snow. The amount of snow that fell wouldn't have been a problem in Chicago where they are used to snow and are prepared to de-ice an airplane's wings, but since the condition was unusual for Atlanta they were unprepared to remain in operation until the weather changed. Many of Atlanta's residents were also unprepared to prevent their plumbing from freezing and bursting, so many homes ended up with water damage from the flooding that occurred.

Shifting climates will result in our homes being exposed to more frequent adverse conditions. Some types of extreme weather are only extreme if they are unusual. Death Valley, California, doesn't experience abnormal heat waves. It is typical, and therefore expected, for it to be miserably hot. Fortunately a little knowledge and some advanced preparation can help prevent serious damage. By acting quickly with first-aid measures when unexpected extreme weather events occur, the risk of extensive and expensive repairs can be reduced.

Above is a photograph of Muir Glacier taken in August 1941 by William O. Field; below, a photograph taken from the same vantage in August 2004 by Bruce Molnia of the US Geologic Survey.

NATIONAL SNOW AND ICE DATA CENTER/WORLD CENTER FOR GLACIOLOGY "ONLINE GLACIER PHOTOGRAPH DATABASE,"

Part Two
The Effects of Changing Climate

Three

Wind Storms

After one has seen pines six feet in diameter bending like grasses before a mountain gale, and ever and anon some giant falling with a crash that shakes the hills, it seems astonishing that any, save the lowest thickset trees, could ever have found a period sufficiently stormless to establish themselves; or, once established, that they should not, sooner or later, have been blown down.

— John Muir, "The Mountains of California: A Wind-storm in the Forests"

A 1935 dust storm approaching a Kansas town.

Wind and water damage from severe storms, hurricanes and tornados are immediate devastating events that traditionally affect certain parts of the country. Tornado Alley, in the central part of the United States, is well known for the twisters that occur there. Hurricanes are typically thought of as Gulf and lower East Coast events. It appears these types of storms are increasing in intensity, duration, frequency and location.

39

Climate Change Effects

The shift in climate is making it more common to hear of uncommon events, in places that have not been frequently affected. Until recently, there has never been a hurricane recorded in the South Atlantic. According to a NASA report:

> ... on Sunday morning, March 28th, 2004, a storm struck the Brazilian coast that ... forecasters believe ... to be the first hurricane ever recorded in that region of the world. The unnamed storm made landfall near the town of Torres just south of the resort town of Laguna · in the southern Brazilian state of Santa Catering, about 500 miles south of Rio de Janeiro. There were reports of winds as high as 100 kph (62 mph) in the area. So far, reports indicate that two people were killed by the storm with 500 homes destroyed and 20,000 homes damaged. This event left 1,500 people homeless.

South Atlantic hurricanes have been so rare that this hurricane remains officially unnamed (NASA, TRMM).

Another rare event occurred when tropical storm John formed in the eastern Pacific Ocean on August 28, 2006. It didn't make landfall as a hurricane in southeastern Baja California until September 1. Eastern Pacific Ocean hurricanes have previously occurred, but the 2006 hurricane season had appeared much more threatening to the west coast than usual. The United States was not significantly impacted by hurricane John; however, the west coast of Mexico had significant impact to many of their tourist beach communities (NASA, Hurricane Archives).

The extreme or violent nature of tornados and hurricanes has resulted in improved tracking and monitoring systems being developed for those areas where they are common. Hurricanes are generally monitored by satellites which can keep an eye on

"Impacts due to altered frequencies and intensities of extreme weather, climate, and sea level events are very likely to change."

(IPCC 2007 page 14
Summary for Policymakers)

most parts of our planet, but smaller, more localized events like tornados still require visual confirmation, which results in much shorter advanced notifications. The National Oceanic Atmospheric Administration (NOAA) constantly monitors these events and issues a variety of Hazardous Weather Outlook notifications. The amount of advance warning notification varies, ranging from a few minutes to several days, depending on the type of weather condition and whether meteorologists are prepared to look for the event in that area. As forecasting gets better, these advanced notifications are helping to save lives and property.

Thunderstorms are frequently a warning sign for a number of other types of weather events. In his book *The Weather Makers,* Australian scientist Tim Flannery tells us that all hurricanes start with a "mere thunderstorm" and must have a "particular configuration of atmospheric conditions" that help "transform growing thunderstorms into more potent weather events" (Flannery). The more extreme weather that can develop from thunderstorms includes lightning, hail, tornados and hurricanes.

Wind Storms

Hot moist air travels toward colder areas. This is one of the factors that results in moisture coming from the warm water Gulf of Mexico into the United States, east of the Rocky Mountains, and explains why humidity levels tend to be highest in southern states. As a warm air front contacts cold air the energy released can result in wind storms. When considering damage to our homes, it may not matter much whether the thunderstorm activity results in a twister or strong wind gusts

Wind creates a number of powerful forces that can damage houses.

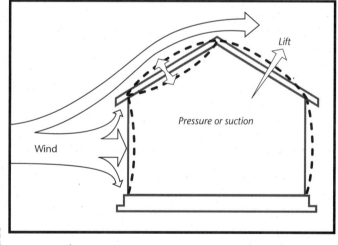

SIMPSON STRONG-TIE CO. INC

from severe weather cells that can reach speeds of 80 to 125 miles-per-hour. "In a severe thunderstorm, wind damage is generally noted in only one direction, with all trees being pushed to the ground one way. In the tightly spiraling and counterclockwise rotation typical of a tornado, however, trees may be mowed down in one direction on one side of the street while being toppled in the opposite direction on the other side of the tornado's funnel. That's precisely the distinguishing characteristic that post-storm investigative meteorologists study on a site visit the day after" (Jakobsen).

Improving structures' wind resistance is an important step in preventing this damage. This has been especially important in parts of the country that historically have been subjected to extreme weather events, but may be becoming more important for other areas of the country as well. The recommendations in this chapter for preparing for wind-related extremes apply to all wind events. Some additional recommendations for homes at risk for tornados and hurricanes will be discussed in their specific chapters.

Roof Uplift

The same forces that allow airplanes to fly are exerted on roofs exposed to strong winds. The angle of your roof can make a great difference to whether your roof will stay intact or sail away like the wings of a plane. Research conducted by Clemson University at their wind load test facility has demonstrated that a category 5 hurricane can develop uplift as much as 100-pounds-per-square-foot. This is typically enough to lift a house right off its foundation. The lifting force is greatest for flat or low-slope roofs. As the angle of the roof increases the force drops. A roof slope between 4.5 and 6.5 seems to be the least aerodynamic. A gable roof will act more like the wings of a plane than a hip roof which slopes down on all sides, helping to cancel lift forces from all directions (Clemson).

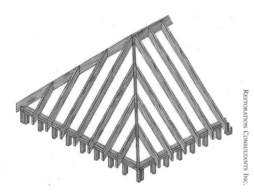

RESTORATION CONSULTANTS INC.

Hipped roofs slope down on all sides creating less wind resistance and uplift.

The lifting force of wind is tremendous. When airplanes taxi for takeoff they achieve speeds in the 50 to 150 mph range, which is about the same as those speeds found in damaging winds. The roof of your home has a much greater lifting surface area than most airplane wings, allowing the entire roof to be lifted off the house. Once the roof is gone the walls will easily collapse. The lifting force for a roof — just like an airplane wing — is caused by the Bernoulli effect of air passing over the top of the roof creating lift. Some people have advised keeping your windows open to help neutralize the interior building pressure but this doesn't really work and will let in lots of water causing additional damage to the interior. The best way to keep homes intact when exposed to strong winds is to keep them in one piece and securely fixed to the foundation.

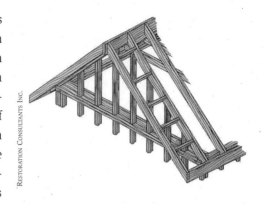

Gable roofs have greater wind resistance on the vertical ends. Additional attic bracing for the gable end walls can reduce damage risk.

Intricate roofs or those with numerous valleys and changes in pitch are more likely to leak when wind-driven rain forces the water under the flashing or roofing materials or when roofing shingles are blown off. The roofing shingles near the roof edge, which faces the worst winds, should be set in special mastic during construction or re-shingling. Don't run a solid line of mastic, use dabs so if water does get under the shingles, it will be able to drain back out. Try to eliminate or minimize penetrations through the roof with special louvered storm vents instead of the standard types of ventilation vents. Roof overhangs help protect walls against water intrusion much better than zero clearance overhangs.

Whole-house strapping is made up of metal fasteners that are important for tying the building together. The ties should be installed at stress points for load-bearing walls. Securing non-load-bearing walls adds extra expense without significantly improving the durability of the home. Experience has demonstrated that many of the homes with the greatest damage weren't fastened at the critical junctions between the roof and the walls, the upper and lower floors and the walls to the foundation.

Various anchors and ties can be used to create a continuous load path from the foundation to the roof.

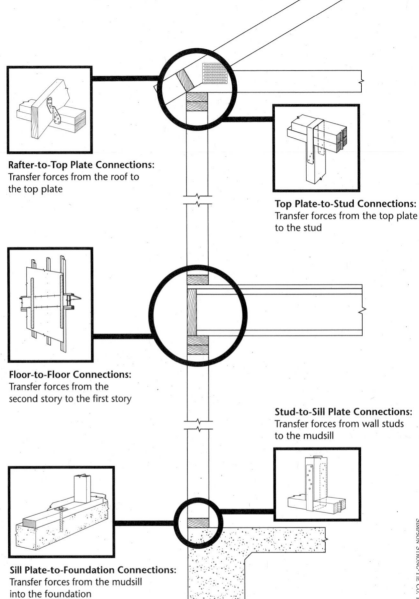

Rafter-to-Top Plate Connections: Transfer forces from the roof to the top plate

Top Plate-to-Stud Connections: Transfer forces from the top plate to the stud

Floor-to-Floor Connections: Transfer forces from the second story to the first story

Stud-to-Sill Plate Connections: Transfer forces from wall studs to the mudsill

Sill Plate-to-Foundation Connections: Transfer forces from the mudsill into the foundation

SIMPSON STRONG-TIE CO. INC

Many times people believe their wall sill plates are bolted to the foundation, but find out differently once the house has been blown off the foundation. Since the foundation bolts are generally hidden in wall cavities, inspecting them is a little more difficult, but can usually be accomplished by drilling a three-eighth-inch hole for a boroscopic inspection. If you have an unfinished attached garage, it may be easy to determine if foundation bolts are present. If the bolts are seen in the garage, it is likely they will also be present for the rest of the house. If the bolts are missing in the garage then the boroscope should be used to make a determination for the rest of the house.

Doors should be well supported with a minimum of three hinges and deadbolts for exterior doors. Patio doors are at great risk; they should be made up of impact-resistant materials and protected with shutters that are also impact resistant. One of the most common forms of damage from any form of high wind is to the garage door. If the garage door fails it is more likely for the garage to be blown away from the house. If the garage is attached to the house and supporting a part of the roof, the house is more likely to collapse if the garage fails and pulls the roof down with it. If the garage supports the rest of the house you may want to retrofit so the home won't be as likely to collapse if the garage is torn away. This should be designed into plans for new construction.

Special reinforced doors are available, and no garage door should span more than eight feet. Garage door reinforcing kits can be used to retrofit existing garage doors.

TESTO, INC.

A fiber optic boroscope can be used to examine the hidden anchoring system in a wall cavity. A small hole is drilled to permit access for the scope.

NOAA, SPRINGFIELD, MO

This house was relatively undamaged until it was blown off its foundation due to an inadequate connection between the walls and the sill plate.

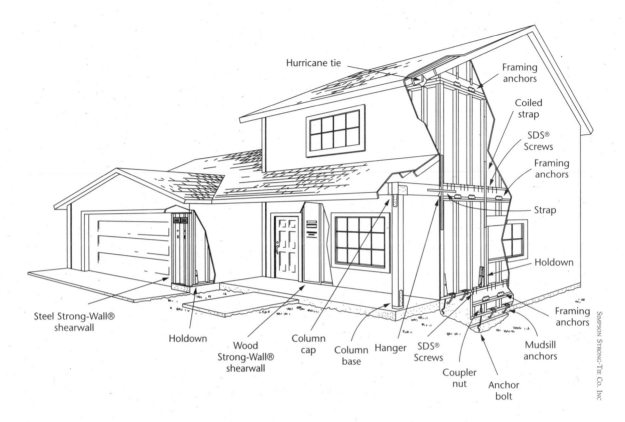

Hurricane tie

Framing anchors

Coiled strap

SDS® Screws

Framing anchors

Strap

Holdown

Steel Strong-Wall® shearwall

Holdown

Wood Strong-Wall® shearwall

Column cap

Column base

Hanger

SDS® Screws

Coupler nut

Anchor bolt

Mudsill anchors

Framing anchors

SIMPSON STRONG-TIE CO. INC

A variety of fasteners are available to significantly increase a home's ability to withstand a variety of extreme weather events.

Several factors are also important for the property around the house. Make sure the home has good drainage away from the building. If water is pooled around the structure, high winds can force that water up into the home's foundation or walls. Avoid landscaping and ornaments that can become damaging projectiles when they are picked up by strong winds. These would include such objects as nearby trees and limbs, lawn ornaments, patio furniture and gravel or rock landscaping.

What You Can Do

- Choose or construct roofs with a good slope to help cancel lifting forces.

- Choose or construct plain roofs. Avoid fancy roofs with lots of changes in elevation and valleys.

- Choose or construct hip roofs for greater structural stability and strength.

- Reinforce the end walls for gable type roofs.

- At a minimum, the leading edge of the roofing materials should be anchored with special adhesive to help resist being torn from the roof. Since winds may come from a variety of directions it is best to secure the edge of the roof all the way around the building.

- Strap the roof to the load-bearing walls and at all joints that might pull apart.

- Strap the upper and lower stories together for multi-level homes.

- Make sure anchor bolts are placed approximately every four feet along the foundation, closer if required by code.

- Use shutters to help protect windows from flying objects; however, even with shutters, shatter resistant glass should be considered.

- Install sturdy secure doors with a minimum of three hinges and a deadbolt lock.

- Check your garage door to be sure it is sturdy enough to withstand high winds.

- Consider reinforcing attached garages.

The house was undamaged by wind until a large tree was blown over.

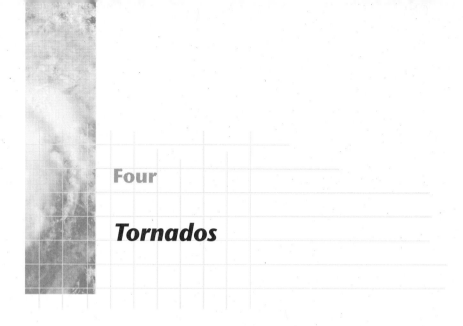

Four

Tornados

Any idiot can face a crisis — it's this day-to-day living that
wears you out.

— Chekhov

Tornados develop from thunderstorms. "… most tornadoes are related to the strength of a thunderstorm, and thunderstorms normally gain most of their energy from solar heating and latent heat released by the condensation of water vapor" (NOAA, Tornado Climatology). This is especially common in areas where cold air from the Arctic meets the warmer air coming up from the Gulf of Mexico. This area is commonly called "Tornado Alley" and forms a belt stretching north from central Texas to northern Iowa, and from central Kansas and Nebraska east to western Ohio. Tornados, however, can occur almost anywhere. Historically the United States has more tornados than anywhere else on the planet. The National Oceanic and Atmospheric Administration (NOAA) also states: "Interestingly, the places that receive the most frequent tornados are also

This is the oldest known photograph of a tornado, taken 22 miles southwest of Howard, South Dakota, on August 28, 1884.

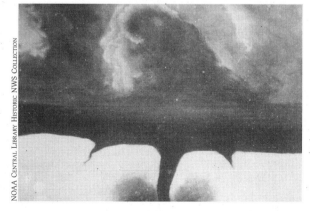

NOAA CENTRAL LIBRARY HISTORIC NWS COLLECTION

Fujita Tornado Damage Scale

Developed in 1971 by T. Theodore Fujita of the University of Chicago

SCALE	WIND ESTIMATE *** (MPH)	TYPICAL DAMAGE
F0	< 73	**Light damage.** Some damage to chimneys; branches broken off trees; shallow-rooted trees pushed over; sign boards damaged.
F1	73-112	**Moderate damage.** Peels surface off roofs; mobile homes pushed off foundations or overturned; moving autos blown off roads.
F2	113-157	**Considerable damage.** Roofs torn off frame houses; mobile homes demolished; boxcars overturned; large trees snapped or uprooted; light-object missiles generated; cars lifted off ground.
F3	158-206	**Severe damage.** Roofs and some walls torn off well-constructed houses; trains overturned; most trees in forest uprooted; heavy cars lifted off the ground and thrown.
F4	207-260	**Devastating damage.** Well-constructed houses leveled; structures with weak foundations blown away some distance; cars thrown and large missiles generated.
F5	261-318	**Incredible damage.** Strong frame houses leveled off foundations and swept away; automobile-sized missiles fly through the air in excess of 100 meters (109 yds); trees debarked; incredible phenomena will occur.

"***Do not use F-scale winds literally. These precise wind speed numbers are actually guesses and have never been scientifically verified. Different wind speeds may cause similar-looking damage from place to place -- even from building to building. Without a thorough engineering analysis of tornado damage in any event, the actual wind speeds needed to cause that damage are unknown."
Source: National Oceanic Atmospheric Administration: www.spc.noaa.gov/faq/tornado/f-scale.html Downloaded 9/16/06

NOAA

NOAA, National Weather Service Forecast Office, Washington, D.C.

F1 tornado damage to the roof and side of a large home for retired priests.

National Weather Service Forecast Office, Philadelphia

Pieces of wood become deadly projectiles as seen by the damage to this garage door caused by an F2 tornado. Amazingly, the flower pot and flowers suffered little damage.

NOAA, National Weather Service Forecast Office, Wilmington OH

Note the narrow path of damage from this F4 tornado.

NOAA, National Weather Service Forecast Office, Birmingham AL

F3 tornado damage to house in the center of image.

NOAA Online World Collection

Note how the house was swept clean off the foundation in this F5 tornado. Some debris is seen in the basement.

considered the most fertile agricultural zones of the world. This is due in part to the high number of thunderstorms delivering much needed precipitation to these areas" (NOAA, Tornado Climatology).

Thunderstorm activity provides the necessary lifting force from warm moisture-laden air. This same principle produces both tornados and hurricanes, but tornados are on a smaller, more localized scale. The tornado forms when hot winds meet cooler air to form a vortex. This results in a spiraling updraft rising up into the clouds forming the characteristic anvil-shaped thunderhead cloud. The warm moist air is less dense and creates a strong updraft within the denser cold air. The large mass of spinning air in the cloud results in a more compact tornado funnel that drops to the ground. North America has historically averaged about 1,100 tornados a year with 90 percent of them occurring in the United States. The other 100 are primarily in Canada.

Climate Change Effects

It appears that tornados and hurricanes are beginning to appear more frequently in Mexico. Researchers at the National Oceanic and Atmospheric Administration have reported what they believed to be a rare tornado occurring in Mexico in March of 2000. "Because of the remote desert terrain west of Ciudad Acuna, the lack of population, and the lack of tornado verification in Mexico, we may never know if there was truly a tornado there. In the US, however, low level mesocyclones this strong are not usually seen even in many storms which *do* produce tornados. Based on all the radar signatures, the best we can say for now is that this supercell *probably* produced a significant tornado in Mexico" (NOAA). In 2006 several hurricanes occurred off the west coast of Mexico, providing more evidence of climate shifts.

What You Can Do

It is not possible to protect an above-ground home from a direct hit by a tornado. The pressure drop that occurs with a direct hit will literally cause the building to implode. For a long time people were told to open their windows to help neutralize the pressure to prevent this from happening. It has now been determined that this does not work. Fortunately the chances of having a direct hit are very low. Most buildings that are badly damaged by tornados are within a few hundred yards of its path and are struck with debris or severe winds. Water damage from the accompanying thunderstorm activity is also a frequent problem.

The roof is frequently the first part of the home to fail. The same advice for securing the roofs, walls and foundations with metal fasteners and bracing applies for tornados as for severe winds. If the roof is torn off the building, the walls are likely to collapse from a loss of structural support.

All of the recommendations for wind apply to tornados, plus the following.

- Attach roofing materials securely and pay special attention to securing the leading edge of the building against high winds from tornados. The leading edge is usually the southwest side since tornados generally travel from the southwest to the northeast. Most North American tornados spin counterclockwise although some with clockwise rotations have been documented.

- Seal all roof underlayment seams with a peel and stick watertight membrane. Make sure the roof has full underlayment and is not merely secured to batten boards.

- Tornado-safe rooms are now available for new construction. For existing homes a tornado-safe room is most easily added in the garage, although this is the most likely part of the building to collapse. Below-ground rooms are generally the safest although heavy duty above-ground units are also available.

- A tornado watch means conditions are present for tornados to possibly form. During tornado watches you can spend time securing your property, but remain vigilant. In most cases there is less than 20 minutes warning that a tornado is on the way. Be prepared to head immediately for your nearby shelter as soon as the watch turns into a warning since this means funnel clouds have been sighted. (The best way to access tornado watches is to have a Weather Alert Radio. These work as a regular AM/FM radio most of the time, but automatically switch to the All-Hazards Civil Alert mode whenever an alert is issued. The radio can be set to "standby/off," but will automatically come on when an alert is issued.)

Five

Hurricanes

Knowing that, if you said "the wind did it," it's coming out of the company's pocketbook, but if you say "it was water," then it comes out of the taxpayers' pocketbook, ... under this system, we have given the insurance companies the opportunity to stick it to the government every time there was a question, and I think they did.

— Rep. Gene Taylor, D-Miss.,
speaking post-Katrina

Hurricane John off the coast of Mexico. Hurricanes rarely develop in this area, but there were several in 2006.

Hurricanes develop from tropical storms when groups of thunderstorms form a vortex. For a tropical storm to develop the energy necessary to become a hurricane it needs warm water like that found in the tropics and the Gulf of Mexico. The minimum water temperature that can support a hurricane is 78°F. According to the first law of thermodynamics, energy can't be created or destroyed; it can only change form. When liquid water becomes a gas it stores huge amounts of energy. When that water vapor again becomes a liquid, it unleashes that energy, which helps to fuel the hurricane's destructive winds. Hurricanes are driven by the extra heat energy found in the tropical ocean waters.

Climate Change Effects

Projected inland penetration for 65 knot or greater winds when a maximum hurricane wind speed of 135 knots and 24-knot velocity of advance strikes the US Atlantic coast.

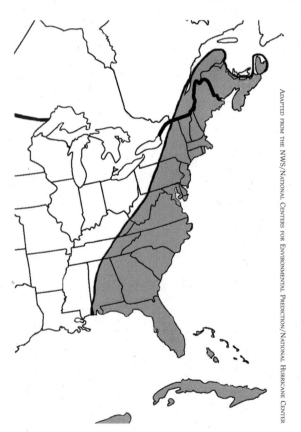

According to Tim Flannery in *The Weather Makers* both "ozone depletion and greenhouse gas accumulation are changing the energetics of the tropopause" (where the troposphere and stratosphere meet) "in ways that can affect hurricane formation" (Flannery). The exact mechanisms aren't clear, and natural cycles prevent making a clear connection with the increases that are presently being observed, but according to a September 2005 article in *Science* there is evidence that, in looking at 35 years of data, "a large increase was seen in the number and proportion of hurricanes reaching categories 4 and 5" (Webster).

Tropical storms and hurricanes are named following the letters of the alphabet. In 2005 there were so many of these extreme weather events that meteorologists ran out of pre-assigned names; the remaining storms were named after the Greek alphabet. This is the first time this has happened since hurricanes began being named. Not only are more of these storms forming but their ferocity also appears to be increasing. Some of the recent hurricanes such as Charley (August 2004), Ivan (September 2004) and Francis (September 2004) have overlapped paths damaging some buildings more than once.

On August 29, 2005, about the middle of the hurricane season, which typically runs from June 1st to November 30th, hurricane Katrina hit the Gulf Coast. Within two days 80 percent of New

ADAPTED FROM THE NWS/NATIONAL CENTERS FOR ENVIRONMENTAL PREDICTION/NATIONAL HURRICANE CENTER

Orleans was flooded, with some homes under fourteen feet of water because the levees were breached. When homes are built on low-lying areas that must rely on aging dikes and levees, they are at a much greater risk than when built in less precarious areas. The magnitude of the disaster resulting from Katrina was so massive that first-aid measures for the hardest hit areas were useless. I visited New Orleans fourteen months after the disaster and in spite of my experience working with damaged buildings I was still amazed at the remaining devastation. The Army Corp of Engineers had temporarily repaired the broken levee I visited. The homes in the area had remained flooded for weeks while the levee was repaired. Entire neighborhoods were decimated and many people have never been able to return to their homes because they no longer exist. The damage from Katrina was extreme and more extreme disasters are likely to occur as the global climate crisis continues.

What You Can Do

Hurricanes present more challenges than high winds and tornados because they are loaded with huge amounts of water. All of the recommendations for protecting your structure from extreme wind should

Adapted from the NWS/National Centers for Environmental Prediction/National Hurricane Center

Projected inland penetration for 65 knot or greater winds when a maximum hurricane wind speed of 135 knots and 24-knot velocity of advance strikes the US Gulf Coast.

Restoration Consultants Inc.

After Hurricane Katrina caused levees to break, this New Orleans home floated off its foundation.

be followed for hurricanes with an even greater attention to detail for preventing water intrusion through windows, doors and other penetrations. Fortunately the hurricane warning system provides a much longer advance alert than is available for wind storms and tornados. Providing you are ready, this will allow you to attend to last-minute details prior to the storm, but don't wait for the last minute to purchase or install the protection.

Saffir-Simpson Hurricane Scale

SCALE	WIND ESTIMATE (MPH)	TYPICAL DAMAGE
Category One Hurricane	74-95	Storm surge generally 4-5 ft above normal. No real damage to building structures. Damage primarily to unanchored mobile homes, shrubbery and trees. Some damage to poorly constructed signs. Also, some coastal road flooding and minor pier damage.
Category Two Hurricane	96-110	Storm surge generally 6-8 ft above normal. Some roofing material, door and window damage of buildings. Considerable damage to shrubbery and trees with some trees blown down. Considerable damage to mobile homes, poorly constructed signs and piers. Coastal and low-lying escape routes flood 2-4 hours before arrival of the hurricane center.
Category Three Hurricane	111-130	Storm surge generally 9-12 ft above normal. Some structural damage to small residences and utility buildings with a minor amount of curtain wall failures. Damage to shrubbery and trees with foliage blown off trees and large tress blown down. Mobile homes and poorly constructed signs are destroyed. Low-lying escape routes are cut by rising water 3-5 hours before arrival of the hurricane center. Flooding near the coast destroys smaller structures with larger structures damaged by battering of floating debris.

SCALE	WIND ESTIMATE (MPH)	TYPICAL DAMAGE
Category Three Hurricane	111-130	Terrain continuously lower than 5 ft above mean sea level may be flooded inland 8 miles (13 km) or more. Evacuation of low-lying residences within several blocks of the shoreline may be required.
Category Four Hurricane	131-155	Storm surge generally 13-18 ft above normal. More extensive curtain wall failures with some complete roof structure failures on small residences. Shrubs, trees and all signs are blown down. Complete destruction of mobile homes. Extensive damage to doors and windows. Low-lying escape routes may be cut by rising water 3-5 hours before arrival of the hurricane center. Major damage to lower floors of structures near the shore. Terrain lower than 10 ft above sea level may be flooded requiring massive evacuation of residential areas as far inland as 6 miles (10 km).
Category Five Hurricane	>155	Storm surge generally greater than 18 ft above normal. Complete roof failure on many residences and industrial buildings. Some complete building failures with small utility buildings blown over or away. All shrubs, trees and signs blown down. Complete destruction of mobile homes. Severe and extensive window and door damage. Low-lying escape routes are cut by rising water 3-5 hours before arrival of the hurricane center. Major damage to lower floors of all structures located less than 15 ft above sea level and within 500 yards of the shoreline. Massive evacuation of residential areas on low ground within 5-10 miles (8-16 km) of the shoreline may be required.

The Saffir-Simpson Hurricane Scale is a 1-5 rating based on the hurricane's present intensity. This is used to give an estimate of the potential property damage and flooding expected along the coast from a hurricane landfall. Wind speed is the determining factor in the scale, as storm surge values are highly dependent on the slope of the continental shelf in the landfall region. Note that all winds are using the US 1-minute average.
Modified from: National Hurricane Center, NOAA: www.nhc.noaa.gov/aboutsshs.html Downloaded 9/16/06

"Some large-scale climate events have the potential to cause very large impacts, especially after the 21st century."
(IPCC 2007 page 15
Summary for Policymakers)

It is not possible to completely protect an above-ground home from a direct hit by a hurricane, but there are many steps that can be taken to help reduce and limit the damage. Windows should not be left open since this will permit entry of massive amounts of water.

All the recommendations for wind and tornados apply to hurricanes plus the following.

- Pay special attention to sealing all roof underlayment seams. A peel and stick membrane covering the entire roof underlayment may make sense for warm humid climates, but should be used with caution in mixed-climates and may be a big problem in cold climates with unvented attics.

- If you can safely take the time before evacuating, seal attic gable vents, and use duct tape to seal eave vents and other penetrations like those for clothes dryers or exhaust vents. Don't forget to remove the tape after the storm has passed.

- Because of the longer warning time for hurricanes, temporary storm shutters can be installed. These can be made of plywood, but are even better if constructed from polycarbonate material which will protect the window while admitting light. The Engineered Wood Association offers a free design guide for window shutters at apawood.org. You will need to sign up with a login password, and then search the publications section for "shutters."

- Seal all cracks and penetrations with a high quality caulk material to keep out water, but always leave a drainage path for water that gets behind materials.

- Below-ground shelters are not an option since they could become flooded with water. The best plan is to prepare the building as best you can to weather the storm and follow the recommendations for a safe and orderly evacuation if instructed.

- The hurricane warning system provides advanced notice of tropical storms and hurricanes that are forming. There is no way to predict exactly which way they will turn, or where they will reach landfall, but there is generally plenty of advance notice for preparation and evacuation.

- Carefully consider that many insurance companies are not renewing policies or are limiting coverage for homes near the coast in areas prone to hurricanes.

"North America"

"Population growth and the rising value of infrastructure in coastal areas increase vulnerability to climate variability and future climate change, with losses projected to increase if the intensity of tropical storms increases. Current adaptation is uneven and readiness for increased exposure is low."

(IPCC 2007 page 11
Summary for Policymakers)

Six

Lightning

> *The reason lightning doesn't strike twice in the same place is that the same place isn't there the second time.*
> — Willie Tyler

NOAA (ORIGINALLY PUBLISHED IN THE BULLETIN DE LA SOCIÉTÉ ASTRONOMIQUE DE FRANCE MAY 1905)

THE EIFFEL TOWER AS A COLOSSAL LIGHTNING CONDUCTOR.
Photograph taken June 3, 1902, at 9.20 p.m., by M. G. Loppé.   Published in the *Bulletin de la Société Astronomique de France* (May, 1905).   [*Page* 82.

The Eiffel Tower acting as a great lightning rod.

Lightning is caused by powerful electromagnetic discharges that occur during thunderstorm activity. Strong updraft winds present during thunderstorms carry water droplets upward where they collide with ice crystals. These collisions result in the top of the clouds becoming positively charged, while the negative charge is transferred to the lower portion of the clouds. These differences in charge result in the most common type of lightning, called intracloud lighting since the electrical discharge remains completely within the clouds. Other types of lightning will discharge when the clouds move through the atmosphere developing a strong electrical potential difference between clouds and the negatively charged earth. It is possible for lightning to travel horizontally up to ten miles away from the thunderstorm activity before striking the earth.

63

Climate Change Effects

Lightning is always associated with thunderstorms. Since climate change is increasing the number and intensity of thunderstorms, it's logical to assume there will also be more lightning. It's estimated there are 1.3 trillion lightning discharges each year. According to the National Lightning Safety Institute, "US government official figures describe losses at some $35 million annually. Accurate information is elusive, however ongoing research suggests realistic lightning costs and losses may reach $4–$5 billion per year" (Kithil). Continued research will be necessary to determine what types of increases in damage may occur with increased lightning strikes. Of course, not all lightning strikes directly cause damage to buildings or utilities; some are also responsible for causing wildfires which can then cause damage to buildings or utilities.

According to the American Red Cross wildfires caused by lightning are usually different from those started by careless people. When people cause wildfires they are typically "surface fires" that burn the surface brush and trees. "A 'ground fire' is usually started by lightning and burns on or below the forest floor in the humus layer down to the mineral soil" (Red Cross). Lightning-related fires may not be immediately obvious and can become well established before they are identified. According to a 1998 National Fire Protection Association report, lightning has been estimated to be responsible for "30,190 house fires amounting to $175.2 million in losses each year during the 1991–1995 period" (Kithil).

The Importance of Lightning Protection

My family moved to Prescott, Arizona, in the late 1980s. Our home was a two-story on high ground near the middle of town. The public utility lines for our home ran along an alley at the back of the property. A transformer on the power pole served our home and our neighbors on either side. Arizona is known for some spectacular summer lightning storms. Since the power poles were clearly the highest point in the vicinity, I was concerned about lightning strikes. Shortly after we moved into the home,

I had lightning surge protection installed at the service panel for our home. Within that first year it proved to be a wise decision.

While our youngest daughter was in the bath one summer evening an unexpected lightning bolt (literally out of the blue) hit the power pole transformer at the back of our yard. Plumbing is typically grounded to the earth, but that does not always guarantee that the lightning will dissipate harmlessly. The house shook, the power went out and the transformer caught on fire, but in spite of my daughter being in the tub she was fine. Many additional strikes quickly followed with brief but heavy rains, typical of Arizona summers. The rains, fortunately, extinguished the flames from the power pole. Other than no power for a few hours and the fried lightning protector that we had recently installed, everything else was fine. Our neighbors weren't so lucky. The neighbor on one side had their refrigerator and some small appliances blown out. The neighbor on the other side had their television's picture tube explode sending sparks into their living room. This lightning was probably a type known as "anvil to ground lightning" since the strike originates in the anvil-like head of thunder clouds. These lightning strikes frequently occur without warning well ahead of the main thunderstorm. This firsthand experience convinced me that lightning and surge protection were important additions and had probably saved our electrical appliances and possibly my daughter's life.

There are additional problems when lightning hits electrical equipment. Power transformers can rupture and leak cooling oil onto the soil below. Coolant oils in transformers manufactured before 1979 frequently contained hazardous PCBs requiring a hazardous materials cleanup when ruptured by lightning strikes. Most utilities have phased out these older transformers and almost all have now been replaced. Many utilities have achieved 100 percent replacement. Your public utility should be able to tell you if your transformer contains PCBs, based on its location. If they are not sure you may be able to use a pair of binoculars and tell them the serial number, which is frequently visible on the side of the transformer, or request that a utility technician check it out.

Lightning strikes can also damage submersible water pumps for wells. Lightning striking close to the well can cause the pump to rupture. Many brands of submersible pumps installed before 1979 also contained PCBs. As little as one tablespoon of leaking oil could contaminate a well and the surrounding water supply. If your property has a well with a submersible pump that might be more than 35 years old, I recommend you have it checked to be sure it doesn't contain PCBs, and if it does, have it replaced now before it begins leaking or ruptures from a lightning strike. Water quality testing and well decontamination procedures are available, but are costly and can usually be avoided when it is visually determined the pump is still in good condition. However, a 35-year-old pump has more than served its useful life and should probably be replaced anyway. If you have an abandoned or unused well on your property, it should also be checked to ensure that any PCB-containing

"According to the National Recreation Association the ten species most likely to be struck by lightning are, in order: oak, elm, pine, tulip, poplar, ash, maple, sycamore, hemlock and spruce. Since the expense of removing a large, lightning-struck tree may approach that of installing a lightning protection system, it is economically prudent to protect large or valuable trees from lightning strikes. In addition, protecting nearby trees from lightning helps protect the house itself, as electric current may otherwise travel through the tree to the house seeking a ground. If the house features lightning protection, it should share a common ground with the tree" (Winter).

"Similar to that for a building, lightning protection for a tree consists of these copper components: air terminal points (rods); down conductor cables; copper fasteners; and adequate grounding, usually 10' rods driven into the earth. Grounding is buried while terminals are positioned at high points and cables are installed along the trunk and main boughs with fasteners driven through the bark. Since specialized equipment is required, installation and testing should be performed by a professional lightning protection company to comply with Underwriters' Laboratories, National Fire Protection Association, and Lightning Protection Institute standards" (Winter).

submersible pump has been removed so that it won't contaminate the aquifer. PCB-containing pumps need to be disposed of at an approved hazardous waste facility.

If your home is located in an area where lightning occurs and is one of the taller objects in the area, you should consider a professionally installed and maintained lightning rod system. The principle behind a lightning rod, which was invented by Benjamin Franklin, is to create a pathway for the electrical discharge from the lightning into the ground, helping avoid damage to buildings.

Lightning suppression and protection systems should be installed professionally and according to code to ensure they will function properly. These surge protection systems are similar to what many people use to protect their computer, but the protection is wired in for the entire home. Lightning surge protection is also available for telephone and cable installations.

If your unprotected home has been struck by lightning or damaged by an electrical surge, it is important to have it checked by an experienced professional who can evaluate the electrical system to be sure it can be safely used. Lightning strikes can melt insulation and wiring resulting in conditions that could lead to an electrical fire or electrocution. Bare wires with melted insulation may not always be apparent since the wiring is typically hidden inside walls, attics and other inaccessible spaces. The electrical system may appear to function properly when in fact wires have been destroyed. In this case, the current will be flowing into the plumbing or other ground paths. This condition is known as a ground fault. It can easily be diagnosed by an electrician. Fire and electrocution

GILBERT PAQUETTE, LIGHTNINGRODSTUFF.COM

Trees may act as a pathway for lightning to strike and bridge over to a house. Trees at risk from lightning strikes should have lightning rods installed, especially if close to any building.

from ground faults can be prevented by wiring all the household circuits to Ground Fault Interrupter Circuit (GFIC) breakers. These circuit breakers constantly monitor the amount of electric current flowing in the hot and neutral wires of each electrical circuit. If the amount of electricity is not the same in each wire, there is a good possibility the missing electricity is flowing to ground along a dangerous path which can result in fire or electrocution. Code requires that all "wet" rooms (rooms with water supplies) have ground fault interrupters. I like the idea of replac-

Typical residential lightning protection components.

Typical Residential Lightning Protection System

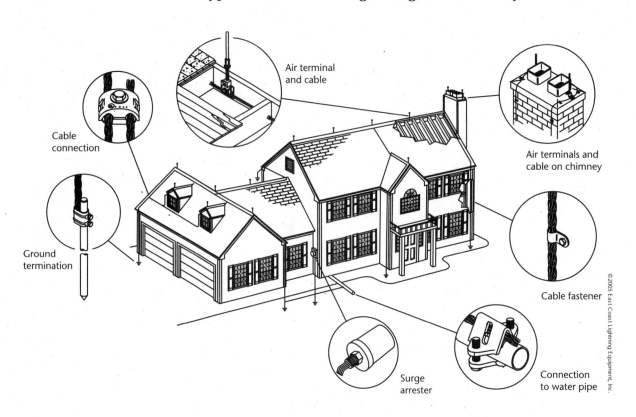

Air terminal and cable

Cable connection

Air terminals and cable on chimney

Ground termination

Cable fastener

Surge arrester

Connection to water pipe

ing all the circuit breakers with these special breakers in a standard electrical box as an upgrade. It is generally a simple substitution for the regular circuit breaker that can be performed by any electrician.

What You Can Do

- Have lightning rod protection properly installed for all buildings and trees that are at risk of lightning strike.

- Have lightning surge protection installed at the main circuit breaker panel for all electrical systems serving buildings in neighborhoods where lightning has ever struck within ten miles. (This means most parts of North America).

- Have ground fault interrupter circuit breakers installed in the electrical panel serving all buildings.

- Make sure hazardous PCB-containing electrical transformers and submersible well pumps have been replaced and properly disposed of and any contamination properly removed.

- Ask your insurance agent if any of the above actions qualifies for a discount on your insurance premiums or a reduction in your deductible for lightning-related damages.

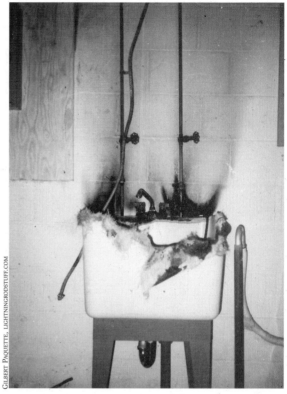

GILBERT PAQUETTE, LIGHTNINGRODSTUFF.COM

Lightning can seek ground through unusual and sometimes dangerous pathways. This strike used the sink's plumbing and melted the sink.

Seven

Hail

The future is already here — it is just unevenly distributed."
— William Gibson

Hail formation is always associated with thunderstorm activity in the air currents churning in that atmospheric layer where the clouds are forming. The formation of large hail requires an updraft wind with sufficient intensity to blow the frozen water droplets upward so that more water vapor condenses on the outside of the hail. If you cut across a hailstone you will frequently observe different layers, almost like the rings of a tree. The clear layers represent condensation liquid that freezes when it forms on the outside of the growing hailstone. The cloudy layers

Damage to windows and a roof from violent hailstorms.

NOAA HISTORICAL ARCHIVES (ORIGINALLY PUBLISHED AS "HAILSTORMS OF THE UNITED STATES," BY SNOWDEN D. FLORA, 1956.)

71

are caused by ice crystals sticking to the outside of the hailstone as it is held aloft by the uplift winds in the thunderstorm. The hail will continue to remain aloft adding more layers until it is too heavy for the air current's forces to keep airborne. At that point the hail begins to fall to the ground.

Climate Change Effects

Extreme weather events involving hail are likely to increase across North America as thunderstorm activity increases. As thunderstorms become more intense there is a greater likelihood that wind intensities will be sufficient to keep the freezing water aloft so the hailstones can form. Historically, the states of Kansas, Oklahoma, Nebraska and Texas have sustained the worst hail damage, but it can and has occurred in every state. When large hail hits homes the roofing material generally sustains the most damage.

What You Can Do

Preventing hail damage involves installing hail-resistant roofing. When you are re-roofing you may want to consider using a more resistant type of roofing material.

Underwriters Laboratories (UL) has established test criteria for evaluating roofs for hail resistance. They drop a steel ball from a height of up to 20 feet onto a sample of roofing material so that it hits the exact same spot twice. The roofing material must not crack from the impacts, although it may dent. Roofing materials that do not have a rating either have not been tested or failed the minimum test. The classes of hail-resistant roofing materials (UL 2218) are as follows:

Class 1 is resistant to a 1.25 inch diameter steel ball.

Class 2 is resistant to a 1.50 inch diameter steel ball.

Class 3 is resistant to a 1.75 inch diameter steel ball.

Class 4 is resistant to a 2.00 inch diameter steel ball.

The test method does not evaluate the effects of temperature, aging or weathering for the roofing materials so make sure you understand the life expectancy of your roof and the warranty that comes with it. You should also determine the roofing materials' ability to withstand high winds and fire.

If you can't afford the extra cost of hail-resistant roofing materials, you may be able to upgrade the roof underlayment to provide extra protection. The roof materials may still be damaged if they are hit with a hailstorm, but the underlayment would hopefully prevent interior damage and water entry.

Hurricane accordion shutters can also be used for hail protection. They have the advantage of being pre-installed so they can be closed quickly and with less danger than if you have to board up the windows at the last minute.

Hail warning systems using Doppler radar are getting better at providing advance notice, but surprise hailstorms still frequently occur. Fortunately the larger hailstones are more likely to be identified with the Doppler radar detection, allowing the National Weather Service to activate notifications on Weather Alert Radios.

If hail damages walls, windows or roofing materials there is a greater chance of rain entering and causing damage to the home's interior. As long as hail damage isn't immediately followed by rain you should have time for roof repairs. If hail damage results in water intruding into the building the water is generally clean, but needs to be dried out quickly in order to prevent mold from growing. Treat this as a clean water emergency water

This large hailstone has smaller stones embedded in it. It's diameter is about six inches — the size of a grapefruit.

NOAA PHOTO LIBRARY

damage intrusion. If mold growth does happen, don't disturb it until you've taken additional precautions to prevent the mold spores from spreading to other parts of the home, and refer to the section on clean water intrusion and mold in Chapter 8.

- When re-roofing, consider having an Underwriters Laboratories hail-resistant roof installed.
- Have hail-resistant shutters pre-installed and ready to close over glass windows and doors to prevent shattering.
- Ask your insurance agent if these measures will qualify you for a discount on your homeowner's insurance.
- Monitor severe weather warnings for your area on a Weather Alert Radio. Weather prediction is becoming continuously better, but it is not 100 percent. Doppler radar can often provide a few minutes' advance warning to prepare your home and yard for severe hail.

Hail Damage

SIZE	UPDRAFT WIND SPEED ESTIMATE (MPH)	TYPICAL DAMAGE
Pea	25 mph	Little to no damage
Grape	40 mph	Slight to major damage to plants and gardens
Walnut	60 mph	Paint and wood dented, extensive glass damage
Golf ball	65 mph	Glass destroyed, masonry walls pitted
Tennis ball	80 mph	Severe roof damage
Soft ball	100 mph	Extensive damage to structures

ADAPTED FROM TORRO HAIL SCALE, OXFORD BROOKES UNIVERSITY

Eight

Flooding

Rain! Whose soft architectural hands have power to cut stones, and chisel to shapes of grandeur the very mountains.
— Henry Ward Beecher

Flooding along the Hudson River, with buildings torn off their foundations floating along the river, early spring 1913.

NOAA HISTORICAL NWS COLLECTION

Buildings are designed to shed water, but not to keep out floods. Floods can be from ground or surface water that flows into a building or from internal sources such as burst water supply lines. Buildings not only suffer water damage from flooding but can also fail when water enters through roofs or wall assemblies when they are damaged.

Climate Change Effects

Climate change and global warming can result in sudden water entry from severe winds, tornados and hurricanes, breaking levees, heavy rains and freshwater pipes bursting from rapid freezing. They may also cause slower events like ice dams and expansive clay soils shifting,

"Heavy precipitation events, which are very likely to increase in frequency, will augment flood risk."

(IPCC 2007 page 5
Summary for Policymakers)

or bursting water pipes from cold snaps. With climate change the frequency of floods is expected to increase. Each of these different types of climate-related flooding and ways to prevent them are discussed in more detail in their respective chapters.

Floodwater entering buildings is going to be either clean or dirty. Clean water can come from sources such as burst plumbing, falling rain, hail, snow or ice. A cold snap may result in plumbing supply lines freezing. The movement of expansive soils can also cause plumbing to burst. These, along with falling rain, hail and snow, are examples of clean water entering a building. Once water has flowed across soil, it is no longer considered clean. When organic material is present it facilitates the presence of dozens of dangerous microorganisms like *E. coli, Salmonella* and *Shigella* as well as parasites and viruses like those that cause hepatitis. Sewage systems frequently overflow, mixing pathogenic organisms with floodwater, creating perfect conditions for the development and spread of disease outbreaks.

We can take some clues from the water reclamation and water damage restoration industries regarding how concerned we need to be about different types of water. Water that is potable (drinkable) is considered "clean" and is generally the easiest to clean up, providing that cleaning and drying occur rapidly. "Gray water" is generally considered to be potentially contaminated with low levels of bacteria or organic matter and may pose health risks. Gray water can be used for landscape irrigation but should never be consumed. "Black water" is grossly unsanitary. According to the Institute for Inspection Cleaning Restoration Certification (IICRC), which has established the *S500 Standard and Reference Guide for Professional Water Damage Restoration,* the category of the water will degrade with time and its flow across surfaces so that clean water can become gray and gray can become black water. In the case of flowing across contaminated surfaces the category of water can change instantly (IICRC S500).

The window of opportunity to deal with clean water may be as short as 24 to 48 hours. Ice damming, for example, generally results in clean water entering into the wall cavities of a building. If the condition isn't recognized and restorative drying begun immediately, the water flows down inside the wall cavity and then begins to move back upward into building materials such as gypsum wallboard due to capillary action. Under the right conditions, gypsum wallboard can absorb water through capillary action at a rate of up to one inch per hour. Mold and bacteria are everywhere, but at normal levels and in a dormant state. When they get wet in the presence of nutrients like those found in cellulose building materials and house dust, mold and bacteria can grow exponentially. By the time the condition is recognized, enough time may have elapsed for them to have colonized the material and caused it to break down or decay. If clean water damage is recognized early, it can be dried and returned to a normal condition before the growth has a chance to become established at higher than normal levels. Normal levels of mold and bacteria are generally unavoidable and do not represent much of a risk; it's when massive amounts of growth occur after water is allowed to sit, or when water is already contaminated from sewage, soils or other contaminant sources, that microorganism contamination from flooding becomes more dangerous.

Contamination and Dangers

During floods sewage and septic systems frequently overfill and spill into the floodwater. Bacterial pathogens in sewage can include virulent strains of gram-negative organisms such as *Salmonella, Shigella* and *E. coli* (Berry et al.). Over 120 different viruses can be excreted in human feces and urine and can be found in municipal sewage (Straub et al.), in addition to a wide variety of fungi and animal and human parasites (IICRC S500). After floods, the use of chlorine bleach can work very well and very inexpensively to kill these types of problem bacteria and virus organisms on building surfaces that are clean and non-porous. This presents a problem, however, since chlorine bleach and most other common biocides do not have a residual action. This allows surfaces to become re-contaminated when outdoor soils are tracked back into previously cleaned buildings. Outdoor soils contaminated with disease-causing pathogens can't be disinfected. The biocides are typically inactivated by the presence of organic materials.

According to research sponsored by the World Bank, when sewage is on soil the potentially pathogenic organisms will undergo natural bioremediation in less than a year. Sunlight and hotter temperatures will speed the process along. A temperature of 114°F for one week will result in 100 percent pathogen death which is an effective process for killing bacteria and viruses (Feachem). Allowing soil to bioremediate for a year before consuming raw food from the garden is a good idea. Proper cooking will destroy any residual organisms. Always practice good hygiene

Anticipated Pathogen Death Rate for Excreted Infections

PATHOGEN	MAXIMUM LIFE OF INFECTIVE STAGE (AT 20–30°
Enteric viruses	6 months
Hepatitis A virus	7 months
Rotavirus	1 year
Entamoeba histolytica	20 days
Giardia lamblia	3 months
Salmonella typhi	60 days
Other Salmonellae	1 year
Shigella	40 days
Pathogenic E. coli	1 year

ADAPTED FROM RICHARD G. FEACHEM, ET. AL., APPROPRIATE TECHNOLOGY FOR WATER SUPPLY AND SANITATION

Viral and bacterial pathogens associated with sewage are unlikely to survive more than a year in infected soils.

by washing before eating, drinking or touching your face.

Pathogens aren't the only potential problem with consuming food from your garden. Flood waters frequently carry chemicals and heavy metals that can contaminate the soil. You may want to consider having your soil tested prior to reclaiming your garden.

When sewage flows into buildings, you can't wait a year. Removing the organic materials and leaving the surfaces clean and dry is the most important part of returning a building to normal. It is important that hidden surfaces also be cleaned to remove trapped organic materials. I don't know any effective way of doing this without removing the gypsum or other materials covering the walls to expose the wall cavities.

Additional dangers may be present in flooded buildings. After catastrophic floods, wild animals, snakes and insects may move into buildings. It is also common for electrical installations in the flooded basement to still be energized. The plumbing may also be carrying current. All of these conditions can be very dangerous. Stay out of flooded areas that are unsafe, if you don't know how to protect yourself and what you are doing.

Unprotected workers face numerous health risks as they salvage what they can after flood waters have damaged a home.

Drying Flooded Buildings

If a building is wet, you can generally see or feel the moisture; however, you can't tell if a building is *dry* by touch. There are meters that can be used to determine when a building is dry enough for reconstruction. Unfortunately, one of the most sensitive materials for mold growth is the commonly used paper-faced gypsum board. The paper material is an excellent food source and the gypsum center absorbs and holds water so that when it is installed

FEMA, MARVIN NEUMAN

over wet wood framing the moisture transfers from the wood to the gypsum board paper and mold frequently begins to grow a few days later. After a ground or surface water flood, wet gypsum board should be removed and discarded. Don't waste time trying to dry it. Once the gypsum board has been removed the structure can be cleaned and dried to prevent further deterioration. The USEPA in their document *Mold Remediation in Schools and Commercial Buildings* recommends that rapid drying begin within 24 hours of a water damage and continue until the building is dry. This rapid response generally is not possible after ground or surface water flooding.

Mold, Bleach and Biocides

Biocides are chemicals that under the correct circumstances kill microorganisms. Chlorine bleach does not prevent mold growth or reliably kill the mold spores. Even if bleach did kill mold spores, which are like little invisible seeds, that doesn't make it safe. According to the EPA in their document *Mold Remediation in Schools and Commercial Buildings:* "The purpose of mold remediation is to remove the mold to prevent human exposure and damage to building materials and furnishings. It is necessary to clean up mold contamination, not just to kill the mold. Dead mold is still allergenic, and some dead molds are potentially toxic. The use of a biocide, such as chlorine bleach, is not recommended as a routine practice during mold remediation" (EPA).

Numerous instances during my career have convinced me that bleach or other biocides are not an appropriate treatment for mold remediation. Yet both the Red Cross and FEMA recommend using biocides such as chlorine bleach as an important part of the cleanup process after catastrophic water losses from floods. This is because chlorine can be very effective for killing disease-causing organisms which are prevalent in flood or contaminated water situations. People misunderstand why biocides are used in these situations. In flood situations the bleach is used as a disinfectant for viruses, bacteria and other parasitic organisms that frequently proliferate after these types of losses — not the mold.

I frequently encounter people who state they used bleach and it was effective in preempting mold for them. The simple fact is they didn't have mold growth because the materials were dry or they do have mold but it is hidden in the wall cavity where it can't be seen without removing the gypsum wallboard. ☛

Pumping out Basements, Below-ground Pools, Spas and Septic Tanks

After floodwaters recede, people generally want to begin the cleanup process as quickly as possible to prevent additional deterioration and to salvage as many belongings as possible. In most cases this is the correct response; however, there are some situations where recovery should be delayed. If you have a basement, below-ground pool, spa or septic tank, pumping the water out too quickly may result in irreversible damage.

RESTORATION CONSULTANTS, INC.

Protected worker in sewage-flooded basement.

Dry buildings don't develop mold. Wet buildings get moldy if they stay wet long enough and the nutrients are present. In my experience, the bleach has nothing to do with the mold prevention.

Cleaning mold off hard non-porous surfaces and performing mold remediation are two completely different things. If you have mold growing in your bathroom on the shower or bathtub tile or the fiberglass enclosure around it, you have a common situation of mold growing on a hard non-porous surface. This is not a serious situation. It merely requires routine maintenance and cleaning, not mold remediation. Studies have shown chlorine bleach is effective in cleaning bathroom tub or shower surrounds (Reynolds), as are a variety of other non-chlorine products. It's even better if there is a surfactant present to help cut through soap scum and grease. Clorox Clean-up combines chlorine bleach with a cleaning compound and is a much better choice than mixing your own concoction. It is important to always remember that mixing cleaning compounds yourself may neutralize the cleaning agent or, even worse, result in toxic fumes. Many people are hospitalized each year, and some die, from mixing chlorine bleach with ammonia.

The only method I have found to be effective for mold remediation, where mold is growing inside wall cavities, or into soft porous materials like gypsum wallboard, involves removing and discarding the moldy building materials to get the growth out of the building, wall cavities or other hidden spaces. The wood framing can generally be dried and cleaned or sanded to remove mold growth from the surface of the wood. Unless the entire building has been damaged, containment may be necessary to help isolate high concentrations of mold spores from unaffected portions of the building. If spores have already spread, special detail cleaning may be needed.

Rapidly pumping out a basement may result in the basement attempting to float. Most people don't think of concrete as floating, but it can be buoyant when the shape is right. As the water is pumped out of the basement the water in the ground pushes the home upward, potentially resulting in the collapse of the structure or at least severe structural damage. The correct approach is to pump out a couple of feet of water, mark the level and wait a few hours to see if the water level in the basement begins to rise. If the water level goes up, it indicates the groundwater is saturated at the foundation and no more water should be removed until the groundwater level drops. If after waiting a few hours the water level hasn't risen, then it's generally okay to pump out a couple more feet of water. Repeat this process until the basement is dry.

This drain and wait process will work for most basements since basements are rarely watertight. Basements stay dry because of good drainage, not because they are watertight.

Below-ground swimming pools and spas will literally pop out of the ground if they are pumped out while the ground is saturated. These usually *are* watertight so you can't tell if the groundwater level is too high based on whether the pool will fill back up after a couple of feet of water have been pumped out. If you can't tell if the groundwater has receded, proceed very carefully and slowly. Although sludge-filled pools are not pleasant, it is best to wait to pump these out until you are sure groundwater has receded. As long as the pool remains full the weight of the water inside will counter the hydrostatic pressure pushing inward from the water in the soil.

The same is true of septic and other types of tanks. Frequently the septic tank will fill up with silt and need to be pumped so that it can start being used again without immediately overflowing. Pumping the tank while groundwater levels are still elevated can result in the septic tank floating upward and popping out of the ground, destroying any chance of an easy fix. In this situation it is probably best to have only enough pumped to

"North America"
"Warming in western mountains is projected to cause decreased snowpack, more winter flooding, and reduced summer flows, exacerbating competition for over-allocated water resources."
(IPCC 2007 page 10
Summary for Policymakers)

provide for immediate use, and then have it pumped out all the way in a few weeks once groundwater has fully receded to a depth below the septic tank.

Both the Red Cross and the Federal Emergency Management Association (FEMA) have jointly published recommendations for dealing with flood emergencies. "Repairing your Flooded Home" can be ordered from the Red Cross or downloaded at: redcross.org/services/disaster/0,1082,0_570 _,00.html.

This information should not be looked at as a substitute for professional assistance, but as emergency information to assist until you can hire professionals. The Institute of Inspection, Cleaning and Restoration (IICRC) offers referrals to certified water damage restoration firms. These companies have drying and monitoring equipment. Their employees have met training requirements. Referred companies have also agreed to comply with the IICRC's code of ethics and have met the requirements for being insured. Referrals are available at iicrc.org.

Prevention and Recovery

There are two general approaches for preventing damage from flooding. The first is to build to avoid flooding. The second is to build to make it easy to recover from flooding.

Building to avoid flooding involves avoiding areas that are likely to flood, ensuring good drainage and raising the structure well above levels that may flood. Although it is possible to raise existing buildings onto a new higher foundation, preventing damage from flooding is more cost-effective when starting with new structures or a site not likely to flood.

Recovering from floods is not pleasant but it can be done especially if the building has been constructed and prepared in advance and you understand the process. In general, you can recover more easily from a flood by not building with sensitive, difficult-to-clean materials and keeping "at risk" furniture and contents off the floor and well above potential flood levels. Some materials are better suited for recovery than others.

For example, you can get paperless gypsum board such as DensArmor Plus by Georgia Pacific. It is far less at risk of developing mold growth since it has no paper-faced material. Paperless gypsum is not the same thing as greenboard, which also has a paper covering that will support mold growth on its green surface paper. Greenboard doesn't fall apart the way that wet paper-faced gypsum wallboard does, but it also doesn't prevent mold growth. Paperless gypsum has a non-nutritive fiberglass facing. Make sure you use the type with this facing on both sides. This product is becoming more popular and available. Our local Home Depot is now stocking it, but many areas may not yet have it readily available and it would need to be special ordered. It typically costs about 50 percent more, but is cheap insurance compared with the cost of mold growth and having to tear the building apart again if residual moisture can't be completely eliminated.

Even if paperless gypsum wallboard was used when a home was originally built, the paperless gypsum that goes below the water line would still need to be removed to access the wall cavities for cleaning out the organic debris, which will rot and smell. The absence of paper in the wall will reduce the likelihood that mold will recur and will substantially reduce the amount of work required to get the building back to normal. It is a lot more difficult and costly to safely remove mold-infested paper-covered gypsum wallboard than just plain dirty paperless gypsum wallboard.

Hurricane Wilma and the Florida Keys

The Florida Keys are a string of islands extending from the southern tip of Florida approximately 120 miles south. The islands are linked to the mainland by a series of bridges or "keyways." The furthest island is Key West. For the most part, 2005 storms missed or only caused minor problems for Key West. Then at the end of October along came Wilma. It didn't hit directly, but many buildings were still damaged. Some of the buildings damaged by Wilma were due to the driving winds, but the vast majority of damage was from the storm surge that flooded over 40 percent of the island. Storm surge occurs when water from the ocean is driven ashore by the winds. The water piles up and engulfs any area low enough for the water to enter. Low-lying buildings were flooded and the deterioration clock began to tick. One of the major problems with the Florida Keys is that almost no part of the over 1,700 islands that make up the island chain have an elevation much over 20 feet.

When the storm surge waves from hurricane Wilma rolled into the Florida Keys they brought an incalculable amount of water and marine organisms, which mixed with the sewage from the sanitary sewer systems and garbage as well as other debris created by the storm. The water flowed into buildings, flooding between a few inches to a few feet. Buildings with crawlspaces ended up with silt debris, seaweed, as well as dead marine life and other unlucky animals decaying in the crawlspace under their first floors. Buildings built on slab foundations ended up with the same types of debris inside.

The residents of the island discovered that a locked door is rarely a match for a wall of water. If the water can't find a path around or through a home it may either knock or float the building off its foundation. Once a building has left its foundation, it can rarely be repaired. The storm surge from hurricane Wilma didn't have enough energy to move many buildings off their foundations, but I viewed some of the numerous other problems when I first visited Key West, about 12 weeks after the storm. I ended up making several repeat visits. I was brought in by clients to conduct some mold investigations and advise them on the water damage and mold remediation process as well as to provide a post-remediation evaluation to help assure the mold levels had been returned to normal. Florida State law requires that water damage to buildings be disclosed as a part of any resale. To help ensure that buildings have been returned to an acceptable condition a mold evaluation report is typically issued.

"Very large sea level rises that would result from widespread deglaciation of Greenland and West Antarctic ice sheets imply major changes in coastlines and ecosystems, and inundation of low-lying areas, with greatest effects in river deltas."

(IPCC 2007 page 15 Summary for Policymakers)

Storm surge-damaged gypsum board and insulation can't be saved, so in most of the buildings I looked at they had been removed shortly after the water damage occurred to allow air drying of the remaining wood framing or concrete block that is commonly used for construction on the island. In those buildings where it had not been removed, the gypsum board was falling apart, full of mold growth, and smelling horribly from the bacteria and dead sea life that hadn't yet been removed and disinfected.

In the cases where the residents quickly removed and discarded the water-damaged gypsum wallboard, they simply left the wet wood framing in the homes exposed to allow natural air circulation for drying. What I found surprising was that even after three months of air drying the wood framing materials and furring strips had a wood moisture content greater than 30 percent. It became apparent that mechanical drying using dehumidifiers and air circulation would be necessary to get these buildings dry enough for reconstruction. Experience has shown that if the wood surface is exposed to air circulation it is rare for mold to grow even if the center of the wood still has elevated levels of moisture. Fortunately, leaving the walls open and not rushing reconstruction avoids the problem of mold growing.

One of the big problems I observed while in Key West were homes where the gypsum wallboard and insulation had been removed and replaced with new materials while the wood still had these elevated levels of moisture. These homes began to grow mold on the paper of the brand-new gypsum wallboard materials.

The purpose of this book is to discuss the methods for preventing or reducing damage, so I won't go into a lot of information on recovering from floods such as occurred in the Florida Keys after Wilma. That information could fill a book by itself. Suffice to say, when buildings get wet in hot -humid environments, it is difficult for them to adequately dry by themselves. Assistance by mechanical drying is typically required. Had the buildings been dried completely the growth of mold could have been avoided. Paperless gypsum wallboard would have been less likely to deteriorate, but moisture control is always the most important single factor.

What You Can Do

- Learn your risk of flooding by searching your home's address at the FEMA website to determine the Base Flood Elevation (BFE). This is the expected height the water is likely to rise to once every one hundred years without considering the effects of climate change. You can search your BFE at: hazards.fema.gov

- Do not place any finished areas of the home below the BFE. Better still is to build six or more feet higher.

- If you already have a finished area below the BFE consider remodeling the area so that it can recover easily from a flood.

- Use water-resistant materials and eliminate wall cavities and other pockets where water could accumulate.

- Use nutrient-free construction materials like concrete block or DensArmor Plus by Georgia Pacific instead of less effective chemical treatments to prevent mold growth.

- Apply non-nutritive parge type finishes directly on block or concrete walls.

- Use backflow prevention valves on sewers and stand pipes.

- Don't install washers, dryers, water heaters, furnace systems or storage tanks below the Base Flood Elevation level.

- Use electrical wiring rated for underwater or install the wiring above the Base Flood Elevation level.

- Use flood shields for the basement windows and doors to raise the water entry level to above the Base Flood Elevation.

- Install and maintain sump pumps.

- Use foundation anchoring techniques to attach the house to the foundation so that it can't float away or easily be pushed off its foundation by flood waters.

- Consider elevating structures on piers if they are near a coast or waterway. Elevated structures should be engineered to be sure the design will be safe and effective.

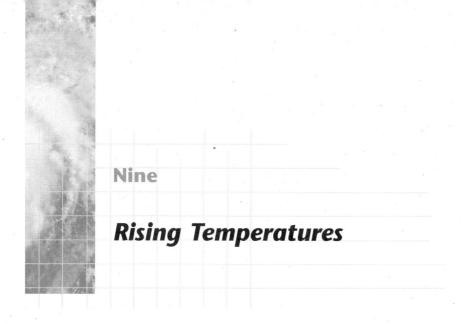

Nine

Rising Temperatures

Nature does nothing uselessly.

— Aristotle

Climate Change Effects

A recent study published in the journal *Science* analyzed atmospheric temperature measurements and concluded that increasing temperatures are widening the tropical zone and have resulted in a 140 mile shift since 1979 (Fu et al.). As these shifts in climate continue, our homes experience effects from rising temperatures that at some point could exceed

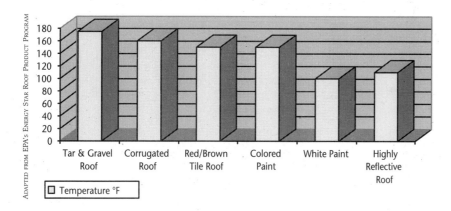

ADAPTED FROM EPA'S ENERGY STAR ROOF PRODUCT PROGRAM

Solar reflectance and thermal emittance have noticeable effects on a roof's temperature. This chart compares these values with typical midday summer temperatures for a variety of roof types.

the structures' ability to function properly by overloading cooling systems and causing a more rapid breakdown of building materials, especially roofing and paint coats.

Heat is a major cause of building deterioration. If the materials are not protected and break down they will need to be replaced more frequently, increasing maintenance and repair costs and adding to the waste stream. Research by NASA scientists has demonstrated that the typical roofing and paving materials used in cities like New York are contributing to localized rising temperatures. "New York City, like other large cities, is warmer than surrounding areas due to the urban heat-island effect, which is defined as an increase in urban air temperature as compared to surrounding suburban and rural temperature. The development of a heat island has regional-scale impacts on energy demand, air quality and public health" (Rosenzweig). The extra heat means construction materials used for homes in metropolitan cities will degrade more rapidly. Much

On warm summer days, the air in a city can be 6–8°F hotter than its surrounding areas.

Sketch of an Urban Heat-Island Profile

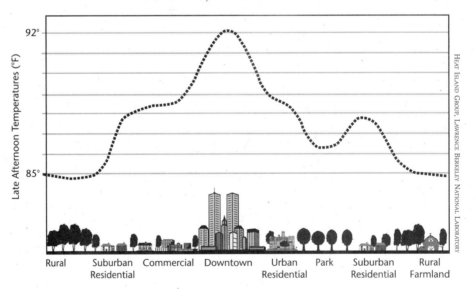

Heat Island Group, Lawrence Berkeley National Laboratory

of this excess heat is caused by dark materials such as traditional flat roofing materials absorbing heat. Not only do our cities tend to absorb a much greater amount of heat, but they also tend to displace trees and other plants that provide natural cooling. Plants help keep the surroundings cool by the process of transpiration which releases cooling moisture into the atmosphere. The temperature in New York City has been documented to be approximately 7.2°F (~ 4°C) higher than is found in the surrounding more rural areas (Kirkpatrick). The NASA study concludes that, "Although street trees provide the greatest cooling potential per unit area, light surfaces provide the greatest overall cooling potential when available area is taken into account because there is more available area in which to implement this strategy compared to the other strategies" (Rosenzweig). Installing light-surfaced roofs and planting trees can help lower the temperature for the entire community, and also result in energy savings and comfort for the building.

What You Can Do

- Plant low maintenance ground cover, shrubs and trees.
- Use light-colored heat-reflecting roofing materials instead of darker heat absorbing surfaces.
- Topcoat dark membrane or built-up roofs with specialty heat reflective coatings. More information is available from Lawrence Berkeley National Laboratory in their cool roofing materials database at eetd.lbl.gov/CoolRoofs
- Encourage your community leaders to adopt community building codes that reduce the "heat island" effect. The model program being used in New York City can be reviewed at: nyserda.org/programs/Environment/EMEP/project/6681_25/6681_25_pwp.asp
- Keep abreast of new developments for cooling our cities through information being produced by Lawrence Berkeley National Laboratory at eetd.lbl.gov/HeatIsland

- Use light-colored paving materials. One promising development is absorptive concrete for sidewalks and driveways. Instead of shedding water it allows water to penetrate rapidly to recharge the soil and discourage flooding from runoff. More information about this product is available at eetd.lbl.gov/HeatIsland/Pavements

Ten

Drought and Desertification

We cannot command Nature except by obeying her.
— Francis Bacon

Drought is a temporary weather condition resulting from a shortage of rainfall which reduces water availability below normal. One short-term consequence of drought is loss of groundcover plants. Desertification results when warmer temperatures lead to a more permanent loss of soil moisture.

"Drought-affected areas will likely increase in extent."
(IPCC 2007 page 5 Summary for Policymakers)

During periods of normal soil moisture, as outdoor daytime temperatures go up the humidity begins to drop. This results in a quickening of the evaporation rate of moisture from the soil. When temperatures drop at night the outdoor humidity level can rise until the temperature stops dropping or the dew point is reached. Once the dew point is reached the moisture condenses and is added back to the soil in the form of droplets of rain or dew. If the temperature drops below freezing the water is added back to the surface of the ground by the deposition of snow or frost which can return the moisture to the soil as it melts.

The areas highlighted on
this map are at greatest risk
of desertification.

ADAPTED FROM USDA

Climate Change Effects

Desertification occurs when increased temperatures result in soil moisture levels being depleted. Since the dry soil has little or no ability to release moisture it can't help restore the humidity balance and there is little or no evaporative cooling. To experience evaporative cooling first hand, compare how much cooler you feel with a wet bandana around your neck versus a dry one. Perspiration is the body's way of aiding evaporative

The National Oceanic and Atmospheric Administration (NOAA) releases drought monitoring maps to indicate current and projected drought conditions.

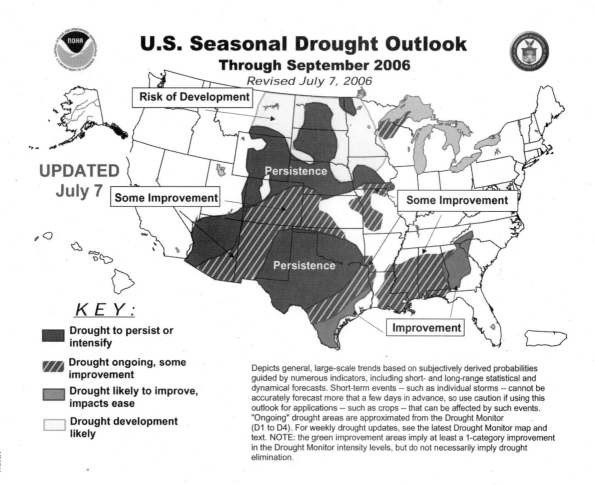

U.S. Seasonal Drought Outlook
Through September 2006
Revised July 7, 2006

Risk of Development

UPDATED
July 7

Some Improvement

Persistence

Some Improvement

Persistence

Improvement

KEY:

- Drought to persist or intensify
- Drought ongoing, some improvement
- Drought likely to improve, impacts ease
- Drought development likely

Depicts general, large-scale trends based on subjectively derived probabilities guided by numerous indicators, including short- and long-range statistical and dynamical forecasts. Short-term events -- such as individual storms -- cannot be accurately forecast more that a few days in advance, so use caution if using this outlook for applications -- such as crops -- that can be affected by such events. "Ongoing" drought areas are approximated from the Drought Monitor (D1 to D4). For weekly drought updates, see the latest Drought Monitor map and text. NOTE: the green improvement areas imply at least a 1-category improvement in the Drought Monitor intensity levels, but do not necessarily imply drought elimination.

cooling. Most building materials have some moisture-holding capacity; this helps to balance the short-term effects of drought as they give off some of their moisture to the interior of the building.

According to Tim Flannery in *The Weather Makers*: "The potential of climate change to spawn drought almost anywhere on the planet is so great that leading climatologists have recently warned that 'it would be a mistake to assume any region is safe from megadrought.' In this regard, it is worth pointing out that the near record rains the United States experienced over the winter of 2005 in parts of the southwest were not sufficient to make up for the preceding dry years, while the northwest remains in the grip of unprecedented drought" (Flannery).

As more areas begin to suffer from desertification, there will be a corresponding drop in the building materials' and furnishings' moisture content. This can result in shrinking and cracking if artificial means of maintaining humidity levels aren't available. In general, wood materials will tend to shrink when the humidity is low and expand when the humidity is elevated. Most of the movement occurs along the width and depth of the wood with very little change in the length. Most materials are installed in ways that tend to help minimize the adverse effects of these movements. For a two-by-four wood stud the change in dimension isn't apparent since the length doesn't change much and the movement of the width and breadth is generally hidden by the wall, the floor and the ceiling coverings. The movement is much more obvious on materials where all the grain tends to run the same direction such as wood floors. Floors don't shrink or swell much along the length of the wood, but can vary dramatically across the width.

Until the climate stabilizes, fluctuations in humidity can be expected to go through cycles of increase and decrease. Many of the changes that can occur from shrinking are cosmetic and will show up as cracks or widening gaps at the floor joints. This is the most common scenario when a climate becomes drier. When a building is built in dry climates, and the climate shifts toward higher humidity, the materials must have the necessary room to expand. If the necessary expansion joints or gaps aren't present the floors may buckle when they run out of room. If this is recognized early, the use of dehumidification equipment may be sufficient to dry the floor and allow it to shrink and settle back into position.

What You Can Do

- Follow the manufacturer's recommendations to allow for shrinkage and expansion when installing building materials.
- Consider using wider baseboards to hide greater expansion and contraction at the edges of wood floors.
- Purchase a temperature/humidity gauge for monitoring the indoor and outdoor humidity levels. Short-term indoor humidity fluctuations shouldn't be a problem, but watch out for high or low humidity extremes that don't resolve themselves in a few hours.
- Use dehumidification to reduce the humidity if floors swell and begin to buckle.
- Add humidity if floors shrink and crack.
- Be cautious of humidifiers installed in the ventilation system. These may be difficult to maintain and may encourage bacterial and mold growth.
- Consider adding plants or water fountains if the humidity levels are low. Make sure to monitor to keep moisture levels ideally between 30 and 50 percent and above 60 percent for only short periods of time.

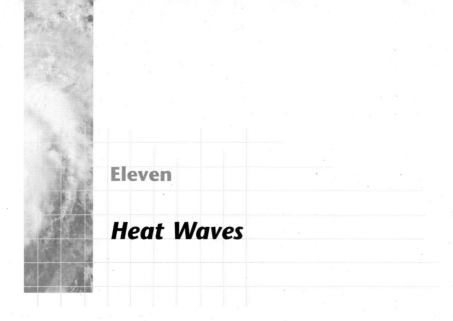

Eleven

Heat Waves

*Ah, summer, what power you have to make us suffer and
like it.*

— Russell Baker

Climate Change Effects

Heat waves are one of the most deadly extreme weather events we
experience each year. About 400 people die every year from heat
waves in the United States. Over 52,000 died from the extreme heat wave
in Europe in 2003 (Larsen). Gerald Meehl and Claudia Tebaldi of the
National Center for Atmospheric Research in Boulder, Colorado, have
used the Parallel Climate Model, developed by the National Center for
Atmospheric Research and the US Department of Energy, to project that
due to global warming heat waves will hit with a "triple whammy": more
frequent, with higher temperatures and lasting longer (Meehl). The summer
of 2006 has been reported as being the hottest observed in the United
States since the Dust Bowl era of the 1930s (CompuWeather). In January
2006, James Hansen, director of NASA's Goddard Institute for Space
Studies announced: "The five warmest years over the last century occurred
in the last eight years" (NASA). The hottest was 2005, followed in descend-
ing order by 1998, 2002, 2003 and 2004.

The mechanisms for extreme heat waves are becoming clearer. Plants take tremendous amounts of moisture from the soil. A recent study by a team of scientists at the Institute for Climate Science in Zurich, Switzerland indicates that the moisture that is transpired by plants into the air is a major help in preventing extreme heat waves due to the cooling effect of evaporation (Seneviratne). A large tree may remove as much as 100 gallons of moisture from the soil each and every day and release that moisture through transpiration up into the air. Plants deplete soil moisture when the amount of water being removed isn't regularly replenished. As soils become dried out, plants that are native to an area may not have enough moisture in the soil to support them without becoming stressed. If the stresses continue for an extended period of time the plants may reach their permanent wilting point and die. At the same time, the shade from trees helps keep the moisture in the soil so that at least it is not evaporating as fast. This would tend to be somewhat of an ameliorating influence. In the short run, plants under drier conditions will suck the moisture out of the soil and dry it faster. On the other hand, when the plant dies, it ceases to shade the soil. The soil moisture is then released more quickly to the atmosphere.

For the most part these extreme heat events in themselves don't cause rapid, direct damage to our homes, but there may certainly be indirect damage as soils dry and shift under the foundation. These will be discussed in Chapter 13. Of course, we need to recognize that higher temperatures will cause many types of materials to break down faster. Roofing materials, for example, often deteriorate as the overall temperature of roofs and attics increases. Asphalt shingle roofing materials have a greater life expectancy when they don't get so hot. Keeping roofing materials cooler is one of the reasons that attic ventilation is recommended. However ventilated attics aren't always better and need to be carefully considered for use in humid climates since the excess moisture may lead to mold and deterioration.

What You Can Do

There are several methods that can help reduce building temperatures and the strain on air conditioning systems during heat waves. These include:

- Follow all of the suggestions already made for cooling cities such as increased planting and using roofing materials that reduce the solar gain.

- Use evaporative coolers in areas where outdoor humidity is low. Keep them clean and well maintained to prevent them from turning into a "swamp cooler." Swamp coolers are evaporative coolers that get dirty and end up growing life forms that belong in swamps, not cooling systems.

- Pre-cool the house each night by using cross-ventilation and fans to exchange cooler outdoor air.

- During heat waves, the whole-house air conditioning system may be overtaxed. Use a supplemental room AC unit to create a "safe room."

- Consider what you will do if there is no power for running air conditioning units. During heat waves, blackouts are fairly common. You may want to consider adding solar power or a back-up generator if medically necessary.

- Learn the operating range for your air conditioner. Many air conditioning units have a maximum operating temperature around 86° to 95°F and become less effective at higher temperatures. This means if the temperature of the air flowing through the unit exceeds that temperature the unit may not be able to adequately cool the environment. Some units have been designed to operate up to 110°F. It is important to know and understand what your unit is capable of doing. If your main AC doesn't work at higher temperatures, you may want to consider a high temperature supplemental unit for emergency use, or as a backup unit.

"North America"
"Cities that currently experience heat waves are expected to be further challenged by an increased number, intensity and duration of heat waves during the course of the century, with potential for adverse health impacts. Elderly populations are most at risk.

(IPCC 2007 page 10
Summary for Policymakers)

Twelve

Fires

As a general rule, the most successful man in life is the man who has the best information.

— Benjamin Disraeli

Climate Change Effects

At its third annual fire congress in November 2006, the Association for Fire Ecology focused directly on the issue of climate change, stating that global warming is changing fire behavior, creating longer fire seasons, and causing more frequent, large-scale, high-severity wildfires that threaten homes and communities. This means the costs for fire suppression and property loss are also increasing due to climate change. It's not that the warmer temperatures from climate change are increasing the fires directly. The temperature increases of a degree or two are melting snow earlier and faster each year. Drier soil conditions lead to a greater amount of dehydrated brush resulting in a longer, more intense fire season each year (Westerling).

FEMA

As temperatures rise soils dry out, increasing the risk of wildfires.

"North America"
"Disturbances from pests, diseases and fire are projected to have increasing impacts on forests, with an extended period of high fire risk and large increases in area burned."

(IPCC 2007 page 10
Summary for Policymakers)

According to the Institute for Business and Home Safety (IBHS), "... nearly every state has been devastated by wildfires in the last century. Over 140,000 wildfires occurred on average each year, burning a total of almost 14.5 million acres. And since 1990, over 900 homes have been destroyed each year by wildfires" (IBHS). Wildfires have typically been considered a problem primarily for the western United States and especially California, but the number of wildfires has been increasing nationwide.

What You Can Do

- Use non-combustible or fire-resistant materials for roofing materials, such as tile, slate, sheet iron, aluminum, clay or stone. "Class A" fire-rated roofs have the highest ASTM E-108 or UL 790 rating and should be able to withstand severe fires originating outside the building.

- Install fascias, eave and soffit vents made of enclosed noncombustible materials and fire-screened to help prevent entry of embers. Crawlspace ventilation should also be fire screened. The openings in the screen should be less than one-eighth-inch square.

- Use heat-tempered glass for windows, skylights, sliding doors and any other exterior glass to prevent early shattering when exposed to fire. Fire-resistant shutters may also help.

- Install exterior siding that is made of flame-resistant materials such as stone, cement block, brick, plaster or stucco. Vinyl siding doesn't burn but it can melt away, eliminating any protection.

- Use quarter-inch fire screen over the opening of every chimney or wood stove pipe. The hot air from a fire can cause the typical air flow to reverse so outside air rushes down the chimney and ignites the interior of the home. Fire screening not only helps prevent embers from your fireplace from causing a wildfire, but also helps prevent wild fire embers from backdrafting into your home.

- Construct overhangs, decks and balconies from noncombustible materials and box them in to help keep them from becoming fire paths.
- Site buildings, decks and overhangs so they are at least 30 feet from any sloped land since fires tend to travel uphill rapidly. The taller the building the further back it should be set.
- Avoid having wood fences attached to your home. They can provide a path for flame spread. Use noncombustible materials to create a fence that will act as a fire break or fire stop.
- Keep roofs and gutters clear of combustible materials like leaves or branches.
- Trim or prune trees so they are at least ten feet away from the roof. Ideally the area 30 feet around your home will be clear to allow fire equipment access. Forested areas should be at least 100 feet away.
- Keep the grounds 30 feet around your home well irrigated.
- Keep plants spaced away from your home, outbuildings and each other to create a fuel break that will help prevent the flames from traveling to your home.
- Trim mature tree branches so they are over 15 feet above the ground. For younger and shorter trees the minimum above-ground height should be six feet. Bushes should be no more than 18 inches high and well spaced to help prevent fire spread.
- Site fuel tanks (propane, etc.) at least 50 feet away from the buildings and keep them well separated from flammable plant growth or other combustible materials. Have easy access to an emergency shut-off valve.
- Store firewood and other combustibles away from your home.
- Access roads and driveways need to be greater than 16 feet wide with 15 feet of clearance to permit access for firefighting equipment, and

there should be more than one way in and out. Turnarounds should be at least 45 feet in diameter and bridges need to be able to support a minimum of 20 tons.

- Have an assortment of firefighting equipment available including a ladder that is long enough to reach your roof and a variety of shovels, rakes and water buckets. Don't take unnecessary risks and know how to use this equipment safely.

- Consider an automatic sprinkler system that can water your home's exterior during wildfires.

- Don't assume your power will stay on for operating well pumps or that municipal water will be available. Ideally, water storage should have gravity feed, solar power, or a backup generator available.

- Specific wildfire retrofit instructions are available from the Institute for Business and Home Safety at ibhs.org.

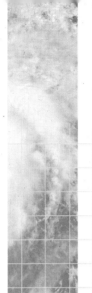

Thirteen

Expansive Soils

A man said to the universe, "Sir, I exist!" "However," replied the universe, "the fact has not created in me a sense of obligation."

— Stephen Crane

Expansive clay soils move as they shrink and swell as soil moisture levels change.

Expansive soils are those types of clay soils that expand and contract when they get wet or dry out. This causes them to swell or shrink dramatically. Whether a soil is expansive or not depends on the type of clay as well as other non-expansive materials that are mixed with the soil like sand, certain mineral salts or loam. Expansive soils expand and contract slowly, based on the amount of moisture in the soil. Still, buildings that are built over expansive soils can end up being as damaged as if they'd been in a typical California earthquake. In fact, expansive soils are

USDA

MG ENGINEERING SERVICES

Shrinkage of expansive clay soil resulted in soil movement and structural damage to this home.

estimated to cost over seven billion dollars a year in damage to our roads, homes and other structures (FEMA).

Expansive clay soils damage buildings by creating tremendous forces of movement. When their expansion and contraction happens underneath the building, tremendous stresses develop in the structure, especially when the foundation is unevenly forced up and down. Even a few inches of rise and fall can have disastrous results for the foundation of a home or building. As the clay soils expand and contract the repetitive motion can crack and heave foundations, crack pipes and pull framing apart. Although this movement occurs slowly over the course of hours or days, it can still pull a building apart at the seams. How quickly depends on how quickly the soil moisture changes. If it is drying slowly, this may take weeks or months. If a tree is nearby, extracting water faster than it is being replaced, stress cracks could start in a few days. At some point, the stress will exceed the building's ability to withstand the force and the material ruptures, forming a crack.

The most expansive clay soils are made up of a mineral called montmorillonite. The expansive clay under homes is frequently mixed with loam, sand and other types of materials that reduce the expansive qualities, but when pure, these soils are powerful enough to generate over 15,000 pounds of lifting pressure-per-square-inch.

To have a problem with expansive clay soils your home, naturally, must be built on expansive clay and there must be changes in the moisture content of the soil. As long as soil moisture content remains within the range of the soil's maximum expansion, expansive clay soils don't move.

Climate Change Effects

As climatic changes from global warming occur and temperatures rise, soils will tend to dry out, resulting in expansive soils shrinking and thus failing to support the weight of buildings. This will likely be a bigger

The potential for expansive clay soils exists throughout much of North America. Shaded areas represent parts of the United States where a risk has been identified. More detailed maps are available at extremeweatherhitshome.com

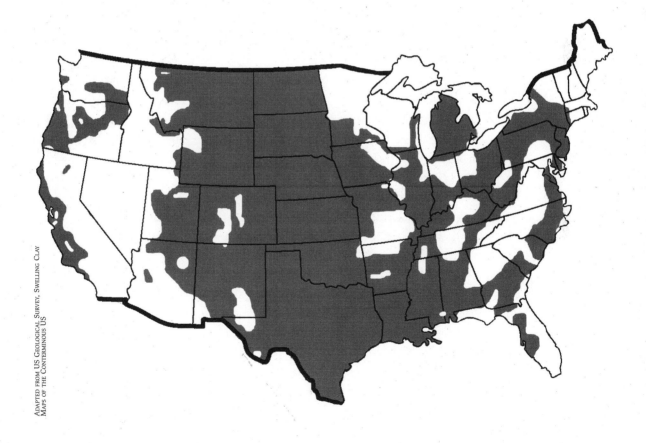

Adapted from US Geological Survey, Swelling Clay Maps of the Conterminous US

Areas with Expansive Clay Soils

The states of Colorado, Texas, North Dakota, South Dakota and Montana have extremely high concentrations of swelling soils. Whereas the states of Alabama, Arkansas, California, Illinois, Iowa, Kansas, Kentucky, Louisiana, Minnesota, Mississippi, Missouri, Nebraska, Nevada, New Mexico, Ohio, Okalahoma, Oregon, Tennessee, Utah, Washington, Wisconsin, and Wyoming have areas that should be checked carefully for expansive soils. The remaining states are less likely to have expansive soils, but it is still a possibility and should still be considered.

problem in residential buildings with shallow foundations than with large multi-story commercial buildings with deep foundations. Even though global warming models indicate increased precipitation, this increased rainfall usually does not hydrate the soil. When expansive clay soils get dry they begin to repel moisture instead of soaking it up. The water is more likely to run off creating flash floods. It takes a slow steady rain, over an extended period of time to restore expansive clay soils to a normal condition. Instead, areas are experiencing periods of drought with short bursts of heavy rains that are insufficient to relieve the drought. This is one of the conditions that I recently observed in Santa Fe, New Mexico. The soils had dried out over a period of years resulting in shrinkage. Suddenly in August of 2006 heavy rains broke the drought, resulting in buildings being flooded, arroyos overflowing and flood evacuations in northern parts of the state. Even greater damage is likely to occur in areas with expansive soils if they soak up the water unevenly and expand. When they dry out and contract repeatedly the risks of additional damage to the home is compounded.

Potential Problem Areas

Many US areas with highly expansive clay soils have been identified and mapped by the United States Geological Survey. These locations of high swelling potential clay soil deposits have been mapped throughout most of the eastern and central parts of the US, and most but not all parts of the western US. Detailed expansive clay soil maps of Alaska, Hawaii and Canada are for the most part unavailable. Expansive soils have been reported throughout the prairie provinces and the western part of

Canada (Hamilton). According to the US Military United Facilities Criterion: "Generally, those areas lying north of the glacial boundary are non-expansive due to glacial drift cover." On the other hand, "areas along the glaciated boundary may have such a thin cover of drift that the expansive character of the materials under the drift may predominate." Volcanic areas such as found in Hawaii are generally not expansive. However, "volcanic areas consisting mainly of extruded basalt and kindred rocks may also contain tuffs and volcanic ash deposits that have devitrified and altered to montmorillonite" (UFC). When higher water tables and colder temperatures tend to keep the moisture levels in the soil more constant, there are fewer problems with expansive soils. Typically, expansive clay soils have been considered a problem in arid regions of the United States. The National Research Council of Canada has also recognized this problem and indicated that "over longer periods of time, cumulative differential movements within a single dwelling have exceeded a foot" (Hamilton).

One of the first steps to determine if climate change may result in expansive clay soils causing problems for your home would be to consult the US Geological Survey maps that detail areas of expansive clay soils found in the United States (Olive). These maps are broken down into areas of high probability of highly expansive clay soils; moderate probability of highly expansive clay soils; high probability of moderately expansive soils; moderate probability of moderately expansive soils; low probability of expansive clays; and areas of the country that have not been determined. For Canada, the National Research Council has indicated that "swelling or expansive clay soils are usually found in lacustrine deposits of Central and Western Canada," and that "in the prairie Provinces alone a million or more Canadians live in communities built on subsoils of very high potential expansion" (Hamilton).

"Even the most stringent mitigation efforts cannot avoid further impacts of climate change in the next few decades, which makes adaptation essential, particularly in addressing near-term impacts. Unmitigated climate change would, in the long term, be likely to exceed the capacity of natural, managed and human systems to adapt."

(IPCC 2007 page 19 Summary for Policymakers)

Recognizing Problems

If the soil is at maximum expansion when a building is built then drying soils can cause the foundation support to subside leaving the building hanging. As the soils shrink around the perimeter a higher central portion of the slab will either suspend the edges of the foundation or the slab will crack and sink. When the center of the structure under a slab remains wetter longer and therefore stays higher, "the most obvious manifestations of damage to buildings are sticking doors, uneven floors, and cracked foundations, floors, walls, ceilings and windows. If damage is severe, the cost of repair may exceed the value of the building" (FEMA).

When trees are planted too close to the building, the roots may grow under the foundation. Since the building shields the soil from rain, the tree may remove moisture from the soil at a faster rate than it can recharge by percolating back under the foundation. A large tree can remove more than 100 gallons of water each day from the soil. As drought and desertification increase, climate change puts greater stress on plants to find water. This creates a greater likelihood that tree roots will remove more moisture from under the building than the soil can support. If expansive soils are present and not kept well hydrated, the tree's roots will accelerate the moisture loss and increase the damage caused by the expansive soils. In these instances the foundation and the tree may both be saved by cutting and capping the roots and re-hydrating the soil. According to Registered Professional Engineer D. M. Robinson: "Research studies indicate that a tree should be at least as far away from a building as the mature height of the tree to minimize the effect of drying caused by the tree" (Robinson).

Buildings with a slab foundation may respond in a number of ways. If the slab has been poured in a number of sections that are not internally well supported, they may respond by raising and lowering at different heights.

As rising temperatures result in reduced soil moisture, tree roots that extend under foundations can cause structural damage. A large tree can remove up to 100 gallons of water a day.

If reinforcing rebar is present they may remain at the same height or at approximately the same height with some cracking where portions of the slab become unsupported or are pushed upward. Different support points may result in the slab tipping and cracking in the unsupported areas.

Damage from expansive clay soils can be especially dramatic in buildings with post and beam supports and a perimeter foundation. The soils may not change moisture evenly, resulting in varying moisture levels in the soil moving the building in different directions.

Preventing Problems

One way of dealing with expansive clay soils if you are building a new home is to dig the foundation to below the expansive clay layer. The depth of the clay can vary. This may require test holes, or an experienced soil engineer may know the appropriate depth for your area. Another is to dig the foundation to a depth where climatic conditions would not be able to cause a shift in the soils by wetting and drying moisture changes. Typically this expansion and contraction won't extend below twenty to thirty feet so this wouldn't be practical for most homes (Jones). Additional protective measures while building a home may include additional supports and post-tensioning the slab. Post-tensioning is an engineered construction method for slabs which involves installing heavy cables in the slab as it is poured then tightening the cables after the slab is cured, to prevent sagging and movement as soil moisture levels change. Movement can still occur but the entire slab moves at the same time to help prevent damage.

A more permanent method that can be used to correct expansive clay soils involves injecting certain types of chemical salt solutions into the soil before the home is built. The salt chemically reacts with the clay to form a non-expansive matrix in the clay. In order for this to work the building needs to be constructed on a soil that has already reached maximum expansion. Adding the chemical salts helps limit further expansion and contraction. None of these are do-it-yourself projects, and all typically require the services of an experienced soil engineer and geotechnical contractor.

Digging deeper foundations for existing homes isn't necessarily a cost-effective building technique to avoid these problems. There are some first-aid measures that can be used if stress cracks begin to form, doors and windows don't open and close easily or you notice a shifting or a slope beginning to develop, or soil pulling away from the foundation. A careful analysis of the situation around your building may help determine the source of the problem. Possibly a tree's roots have grown too close to the foundation. Over- or underwatering may be causing the irregularities. By restoring the soil moisture content to a normal status the soil's movement can be halted and even reversed. With luck, restoring moisture content may move the building back into its normal position. Unfortunately, these forces may have caused nails or other fasteners to pull, in which case returning the building to a pre-movement position may be difficult or impossible. Correcting such damage to buildings is best left to professionals. Many times a do-it-yourself approach will cover up the clues that an experienced engineer would use to diagnose and develop solutions for the problem. Without thoroughly understanding the nature of the problem and the construction of buildings, this approach leads to a costly mistake.

If stress cracks do begin to form and you see that the soil is shrinking from around the foundation of the building, adding moisture back to the soil may reverse the condition, but the way the water is added back can be very important. If you just begin watering the soil where the cracks are

Restoring soil moisture levels may return the foundation to its original position. Applying water directly to the cracks may result in soil washing into the opening, causing over-expansion and irreparable foundation damage.

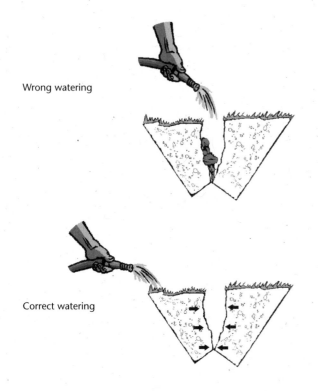

Wrong watering

Correct watering

showing, you will wash soil from the surface down into the cracks. This extra soil will then prevent the expanding soil from returning to its original position by over-filling the opening. By incorrectly trying to correct the problem you may in fact make it worse by overcompensating and packing the cracks with extra soil.

Moisture needs to be added evenly and gradually, and at a distance from the soil cracks in a way that won't allow water to wash soil solids down into the crevices. A soaker hose is one way of adding the moisture back to the soil gradually. Adding moisture back to the soil as a first-aid measure can be done by manual watering but for long-term corrections additional measures may be required. There are moisture monitoring drip-watering systems available that will monitor the moisture level of the soil and add water back as necessary to keep the moisture levels even and constant.

Expansive soils tend not to be a problem in areas with consistently high water tables (these areas tend to have other types of problems with excess soil moisture unless they have good drainage). The soil in an area with a high water table has already reached maximum expansion due to its saturation. But if climate change results in a lowering of the water table and the soil begins to dry out, then shifting of the foundation may follow. A lowering of the water table can also develop when groundwater is being pumped from the aquifer faster than it can recharge. These types of conditions are likely to increase as climate change leads to increased precipitation runoff during short intense rains. This water runs off too quickly instead of being able to percolate down and soak in and recharge the aquifer.

What You Can Do

- Use the maps available from the US Geological Survey and the Natural Resources Conservation Service division of the United States Department of Agriculture to determine the relative risks of expansive clay soils in your state. These maps are only an initial guide. There may be problem pockets anywhere. See extremeweatherhitshome.com for links to these maps.

- Use an automatically controlled soaker hose or drip-watering system to help rehydrate the soil gradually. Watch closely to be sure the soil is taking on the water and that it isn't just running off. The idea is to water the soil to keep it wet enough that it has reached its maximum swelling capacity, but not so much to cause a flooded foundation.

- For new construction consider the extra costs for a stronger engineered foundation such as an engineered post-tension system.

- Keep the soil moisture content as constant as possible around the foundation. During dry periods it may be necessary to add water to the soil. This must be done evenly around the entire foundation to prevent an uneven shift in the soil during extended dry periods.

- Apply water if you discover soil cracking along the foundation. Begin by gently watering a couple of times a day around the entire foundation. Don't allow the water to flow into the soil cracks. Apply the water two or more feet away and allow it to seep into the earth.

- Grade soil to gently slope away from the foundation to prevent ponding of water or erosion of soil. Gutters should direct water away from the foundation. Make sure that swimming pools and other landscape features don't impede drainage or contribute to water collection.

- Watch for cracks in stucco, mortar joints, plaster and where cabinets meet walls. Some cracks are normal for a new building. If repaired cracks keep re-appearing in new buildings, or new cracks appear in old buildings hire an experienced engineer to find out why before permanent damage results.

- Hire a professional arborist to cut and cap the roots of trees where the roots are getting too close to the foundation. You can estimate the area the roots cover by the size of the tree. What you see above the ground is likely to be present underground.

- Talk to a professional to see how to keep a tree's root growth from removing water from under your foundation without killing the tree. During a drought or if climate changes result in desertification, you may need to take immediate action to control the tree. Extreme situations may require removing the tree to conserve water. A full size tree may require 100 gallons of water a day.

Fourteen

Melting Permafrost

Understanding the laws of nature does not mean that we are immune to their operations.

— David Gerrold

Permafrost is soil that has remained completely frozen for two or more years. Approximately 80 percent of the soil in the United States has historically frozen for a part of the year. Building codes take this into account with foundations being required to reach below the frozen surface. As one goes further north, permafrost is present, with the deep soils remaining permanently frozen and the surface soil defrosting at regular intervals. Construction over permafrost requires that the foundation be deep enough so the entire footing that bears the weight of the home rests on soil that remains permanently frozen. If the ice in the soil melts, the home may not be evenly supported.

Climate Change Effects

As climate change results in warming, the permafrost is melting to deeper levels. "During 2003, the warmest

Permafrost monitoring stations have been set up in sensitive areas of Alaska.

ADAPTED FROM USGS DATA

119

summer on record in the Alps, the slushy active layer of the permafrost moved down from its long-term average depth of 15 feet (4.5 meters) to 29 feet (9 meters)" (Britt). As water freezes and thaws it expands and shrinks resulting in severe stress on any foundation that isn't deep enough to reach below the level affected by these seasonal changes. Foundations constructed in areas with permafrost need to be specially engineered, or deep enough have their footing remain on permanently frozen soil. As permafrost melts, buildings are being damaged. "More than 300 build-ings in the vicinity of Fairbanks, Alaska, have been affected by thawing permafrost, although most problems can be traced to inadequate site preparation or design flaws. Permafrost is an increasingly important con-sideration for planners, mortgage lenders and the real estate industry" (Thomas).

This is a serious problem that can easily destroy a building beyond repair. Several options can help prevent damage, but in general they require engineering the foundation to withstand the expansion and con-traction forces and allow the building to "float" with the moving soils. Other measures may involve sinking support piers to shore up the home. These measures generally far exceed homeowners' ability to do them-selves, but some things can be done to help slow or reduce the damage. Homeowners with structures built over permafrost need to monitor frozen soil conditions and know the depth of their founda-tions so that professionals can be called early enough for corrective or protective measures to be successful. The United States Geological Survey provides routine measurement of the active permafrost depths in Alaska. The Canadian Permafrost Monitoring Network provides a similar service for Canada.

Another thing that homeowners can do is make sure the building is well-insulated from the soil so that lost building heat does not melt the permafrost. In many areas the permafrost temperature is already within a degree or two of melting. In this case insulating the soil is most important for maintaining

"In the Arctic, additional impacts include reductions in the extent of sea ice and permafrost, increased coastal erosion, and an increase in the depth of permafrost seasonal thawing."

(IPCC 2007 page 11
Summary for Policymakers)

building longevity, but also pays off by reducing the energy bill. "Engineers are using a simple — and long established — trick of cooling the permafrost with crushed rock" (Bentley). The rock is spread on the soil surface to shield the frozen soil from the solar radiation to reduce melting. Rocks minimize heat intake in summer and promote shedding excess heat in winter. Research indicates that coarsely crushed rock provides better permafrost maintenance characteristics than finely crushed rock (Zhizhong).

The United States Global Change Research Program (USGCRP) has concluded: "While no adaptation options are likely to be available for terrestrial ecosystems threatened by permafrost thawing, or marine ecosystems threatened by sea-ice retreat, strategic planning and research could mitigate some of the potential impacts to the human/ built environment of climate change from thawing and melting" (USGCRP).

"Arctic human communities are already adapting to climate change, but both external and internal stressors challenge their adaptive capacities. Despite the resilience shown historically by Arctic indigenous communities, some traditional ways of life are being threatened and substantial investments are needed to adapt or re-locate physical structures and communities."

(IPCC 2007 page 11
Summary for Policymakers)

What You Can Do

- Determine if you are in an area with permafrost. These locations are primarily in Alaska and the northern parts of Canada. This information is available from the United States Geological Survey for Alaska geochange.er.usgs.gov/poster/permafrost.html, and the Canadian Permafrost Monitoring Network gsc.nrcan.gc.ca/permafrost/mapping_e.php.

- Carefully select your building site. Permafrost with high gravel content is much less prone to heaving. Avoiding permafrost with high ice content and choosing permafrost with more gravel can help reduce the risks of movement.

- Reduce the risk of thawing by not disturbing the surface protecting the soil.

- Insulate the foundation and heat sources to block heat from being transferred into the soil.

- Use longer support piles for the structure. You may be able to sink them deeper into the permafrost to keep the support in the frozen region of soil. There are also techniques for refrigerating the foundation to keep the soil frozen but this is probably not practical for residential construction.

- Pre-thaw the soil prior to new construction. Once thawed it will need to be protected from refreezing. The problem isn't with being frozen or thawed; it's the change between the two conditions. The US Global Change Research Program suggests "stripping vegetation and surface soil from the site five years or more in advance."

- Using gravel instead of paving will result in less damage for roads and driveways. Damage will also be easier to repair.

Rising Sea Level

A child of five could understand this. Fetch me a child of five.

— Groucho Marx

One aspect of global warming that receives a lot of attention is the rising sea level due to the melting of polar ice. As water freezes it expands and floats. Ice floats in water because it is about ten percent less dense than liquid water. Fresh water is less dense than salt water. Ice that is already floating in the ocean is not responsible for a rise in sea level. Only land-based ice that melts is able to cause the levels of the oceans to rise. As the ice at the North Pole melts there is no change in water level since the arctic ice is a gigantic floating iceberg already in the water and therefore not altering the sea level. It doesn't matter if it melts or not because it is already part of the water geography and, as it melts, its volume shrinks. The ice in Greenland is land-based. As it melts the water that flows into the ocean will cause a rise in sea level because it was always locked on the land, and so part of the land — not ocean — geography. When considering sea level rise from arctic ice, the 2004 Arctic Climate Impact Assessment (ACIA)

"Coasts are projected to be exposed to increasing risks, including coastal erosion, due to climate change and sea level rise."

(IPCC 2007 page 6
Summary for Policymakers)

123

stated: "The Greenland Ice Sheet is projected to make the largest contribution because of its size. Although Alaska's glaciers cover a much smaller area, they are also projected to make a large contribution. The total contribution of melting land-based ice in the Arctic to global sea level rise is projected to be about 10 cm by the year 2100" (ACIA). It has been estimated that if Greenland's ice were to completely melt, sea levels would rise by 23 feet. If all the ice on earth were to melt the total sea

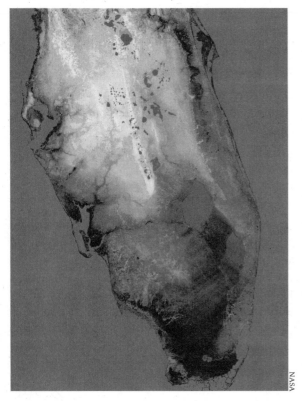

Map showing the present coast of Florida.

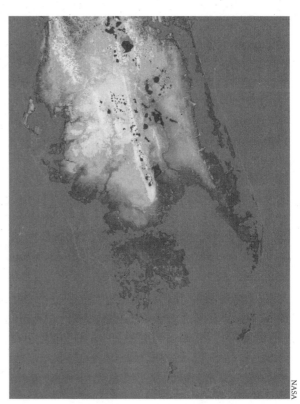

Map showing the coast of Florida if sea level rises 33 feet: a dramatic illustration of how Florida's low coastline makes it especially vulnerable to flooding associated with storm surges.

level rise has been estimated to be approximately 220 feet (Flannery). According to NASA a rise of 16 feet would put coastal communities such as Miami under water. The highest elevation in South Florida is approximately 197 feet above sea level, but the mean is 100 feet (NASA).

In 2002 the USEPA issued its US Climate Action Report. In this report they concluded:

> Looking to the future, climate models project that global warming will increase sea level by 9–88 cm (4–35 inches) during the 21st century, with mid-range values more likely than the very high or very low estimates. ... Because of the long time constants involved in ocean warming and glacier and ice sheet melting, further sea level rise is likely for several centuries, even after achieving significant limitations in emissions of CO_2 and other greenhouse gases. However, these global changes are

"Many millions more people are projected to be flooded every year due to sea level rise by the 2080s."
(IPCC 2007 page 7 Summary for Policymakers)

FEMA

This home is on piers that raise it well above the Base Flood Elevation in an area that frequently floods. As sea levels rise, more homes will need to be raised, expensive levees built and monitored or areas abandoned.

only one factor in what determines sea level change at any particular coastal location. For example, along the Mid-Atlantic coast, where land levels are subsiding, relative sea level rise will be somewhat greater; conversely, in New England, where land levels are rising, relative sea level rise will be somewhat less (US EPA).

Preparing for the Future

Since more than 50 percent of the population of the United States is concentrated close to the coasts there will need to be some fairly aggressive action taken to prepare for rising sea levels. One approach reported by Al Gore in *An Inconvenient Truth* that is being used in Amsterdam is building homes on giant pontoons so that the home can be towed to another location when it becomes necessary to relocate due to rising sea levels (Gore).

Another approach is to build using elevated piers to raise the building well above the Base Flood Elevation (BFE). Everglades is a small south Florida community with many homes raised a dozen or more feet on piers. Water can flow under the raised homes and around the piers so that the force of the water won't displace the structure.

Sandbagging as first-aid for preventing flooding from rising sea level is unlikely to be effective. Sandbagging usually only makes sense for short-term protection. If below-sea level areas are to survive as communities, a massive investment by the government will be required. Levees, dikes and pumps would be required, as various areas in the Netherlands have done. Of course, another option would be to monitor the rises in sea level and move before levels have gotten too high. Existing homes may be able to be jacked up onto a higher foundation as well. All of these measures will probably require extensive professional help and may not be feasible if the local community is abandoned by the government. One of the ongoing concerns

"There is medium confidence that at least partial deglaciation of the Greenland ice sheet, and possibly the West Antarctic ice sheet, would occur over a period of time ranging from centuries to millennia for a global average temperature increase of 1-4°C (relative to 1990-2000), causing a contribution to sea level rise of 4-6 m or more."

(IPCC 2007 page 15 Summary for Policymakers)

that have continued for some of the areas devastated by Katrina after the levees broke is what level of protection will be provided in the future. When I was there in October of 2006 the Army Corp of Engineers had installed temporary levees, but discussion was still continuing as to if a reoccurrence could be prevented, especially if the area is hit by another major hurricane. Other considerations regarding insurance availability and federal programs will be discussed in Chapter 25.

What Can You Do

- Get involved with your local community to help plan what action you and your neighbors will take. Sea level rise is presently occurring, albeit slowly. This is generally not going to be prevented by a do-it-yourself first-aid type of fix.

"sea level rise is expected to exacerbate inundation, storm surge, erosion and other coastal hazards, thus threatening vital infrastructure, settlements and facilities that support the livelihood of island communities."

(IPCC 2007 page 11 Summary for Policymakers)

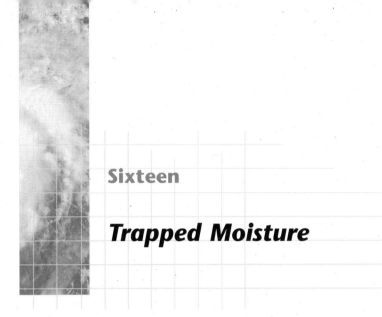

Sixteen

Trapped Moisture

Never, no never, did nature say one thing and wisdom another.
— Edmund Burke

A study of the moisture problems that occasionally occur in houses with inappropriate vapor barriers provides some clues as to the problems that may be anticipated to occur due to climate change. By understanding the conditions that lead to the development of problems, you may be able to apply first-aid measures to avoid damage during adverse periods. You may also be able to anticipate problems and make changes that will better equip your home to resist climate change-induced stresses.

Excess water vapor may result in trapped moisture developing in wall cavities, attics, crawlspaces or other hidden locations. To prevent trapped moisture it is necessary to understand more about moisture in materials, and how construction techniques and maintenance relates to the way modern buildings function. The types

Vinyl wallpaper can act as a vapor barrier, trapping moisture and resulting in mold growth.

RESTORATION CONSULTANTS, INC.

129

of materials used, their application and function can determine whether a building will release moisture (breathe) or retain it. See Chapter 1 for a more detailed discussion of these concepts.

Climate Change Effects

We've already discussed in Chapter 9 how climate change has been moving the tropical zone northward. This has the same effect as taking a building in the north and moving it southward. Each year that the climate shifts our northern cities are becoming a little warmer, and a little more humid. This is likely to result in the northern buildings with their interior vapor barriers trapping moisture during the summer months for a longer period of time. The moisture-tolerant building will be more

How Illinois's climate is projected to change according to the Canadian model, developed by the Canadian Centre for Climate Modeling and Analysis. Its summer climate would become more like southern Missouri's in 2030 and Oklahoma's in 2090.

ADAPTED FROM US GLOBAL CHANGE RESEARCH PROGRAM

likely to make it through to where the season changes and the moisture flow again becomes favorable. As these climate shifts occur there will come a point where some homes will no longer be able to handle the changes and will begin to deteriorate. The buildings that have the lowest moisture capacity (those with metal framing) are likely to be the first to exhibit problems. Wood-framed buildings and especially those built of solid masonry should have a greater resiliency.

Assuming global warming only warms without cold swings, the buildings most likely to experience difficulty are those that have been built with interior vapor barriers in all of Canada and the northern parts of the US. This vapor barrier is helpful during the cold part of the year, but during the summer, especially if air conditioning is being used, the moisture

How Illinois's climate is projected to change according to the Hadley Centre model, developed by the Met Office in the United Kingdom. Its summer climate would become more like West Virginia's in 2030 and more like coastal Virginia's and North Carolina's in 2090.

levels in the walls will begin to climb. Indoor air conditioning may do a great job of reducing the indoor humidity, but won't have an effect on the humid outdoor air flowing into the wall cavity behind the vapor barrier. When moist air hits the cold vapor barrier against an air-conditioned wall, moisture condensation will begin to form inside the wall cavity. Turning off the air conditioner would help save energy and reduce this risk, but as extreme heat waves become more common turning off the air conditioner may result in the need to temporarily abandon unbearably hot buildings.

If warming was all that happened with global warming, then homes in the southern states should be in pretty good shape for dealing with climate change, but that's not how climate change appears to be progressing. Instead, we have swings with unexpected and extreme cold weather events. If you hear that Florida citrus growers have to protect their crops against frost, you can be pretty sure that homes in Florida with their vapor barriers on the exterior of the building will be accumulating moisture in the walls during cold snaps. The warm indoor moisture will try to dry to the cold exterior. When it hits the cold exterior surface of a wall that has reduced permeability, that moisture will also begin to condense and potentially lead to problems if the cold snap lasts more than a few days.

"Adaptive capacity is the ability of a system to adjust to climate change (including climate variability and extremes) to moderate potential damages, to take advantage of opportunities, or to cope with the consequences."

(IPCC 2007 page 20 Summary for Policymakers)

You might think that buildings in the middle, mixed-climate portion of the country would do better than those in the north or the south since they would already be built to withstand fluctuations. Not so. A large number of buildings in mixed-climates have been built with vapor barriers to respond to the energy crisis and are already poised on the brink of moisture disaster. Unless they pay special attention, most people won't know what is going on inside their walls until the problems have developed.

But there is hope. New types of "smart" materials are being developed and will hopefully be marketed before these problems become completely out of control. The ideal "smart" barrier would have a variable permeability that could also change the direction of moisture flow as necessary to accommodate the seasons and extreme weather events. Of course as with any new technology there will be unexpected side effects and there is no guarantee they will work. So you probably don't want to be the first on your block to try new materials.

Preparing for Climate Shifts

I can't tell you how many times I have been called after a bad situation has been made even worse. There are very few problems with trapped moisture that can't be controlled while you get an understanding of the situation. If you do perceive the situation is degrading more rapidly, then use the first-aid measures in this chapter to gain temporary control. If they don't work, what you did was temporary and can be easily undone.

Before you jump into the thick of things and make what may be unnecessary changes, it is very important to learn everything you can about your building and how it should function and respond to various climate events. Joe Lstiburek's website at buildingscience.com, as mentioned in Chapter 1, includes recommendations for construction techniques that should be used for your current climate zone.

Once you know how your building should have been constructed, you'll need to know if it was done that way. A set of plans may help, but are often not available and may not be accurate. Unfortunately, the only way to discover the various layers of materials that make up a wall is to look. This may mean having a company experienced in making these determinations drill a hole through the gypsum wall board in your house and use a boroscope to look inside the wall cavity. The hole usually isn't more than three-eighths of an inch and is easily resealed. It may be possible to drill it in an inconspicuous place or behind a baseboard that has been partially removed. Each material layer and its thickness should be identified to assist in modeling the moisture vapor flow characteristics for your building.

Another very helpful type of inspection involves using a thermal imaging camera. These cameras sense heat and can be used to determine where the cold spots are from missing insulation and air infiltration. These cold locations are likely to be the first spots to fail because they allow condensation to form. Its worth having an energy audit at the same time to determine how the energy efficiency of your home can be improved, but make sure the improvements won't make your home less capable of dealing with moisture. A thermal scan can help predict trouble spots for moisture accumulation in humid summer months as well as problems from ice damming and freezing conditions in winter.

Computer simulation models can help you determine the conditions that will cause your building to take on moisture and those that cause it to lose moisture. Oakridge National Laboratory has developed a computer simulation called WUFI which can be used to predict the moisture flow in your walls based on the construction and location of your building. The simulation lets you choose from over 50 cities in the United States to determine the annual moisture flow characteristics in your home.

Most designers who use this modeling program are assessing current situations. I suggest you use the model to predict climate change problems. Have the simulation run for your home as if it were located in various other cities whose climate approximates the climate you believe your building will be exposed to in the future. Try the simulations for a city one or two climate zones south of your building's present location. For example, Montrealers would run the model simulation for Philadelphia or Columbus. Philadelphians might want to see how their building would fare if it were in a climate like Atlanta. You can try numerous simulations to see what conditions are likely to lead to moisture being trapped in wall cavities and which situations aren't problems. A limited version of the software is free, and various engineering firms have advanced versions they can use to run the simulations for you for a fee. The software download is available at ornl.gov/sci/btc/apps/moisture/index.html. The software can also be used to try out various ideas to see what good or bad may come of them. If you are considering adding an elastomeric coating to the outside of your home, or vinyl wallpaper on the inside, the simulation may change your mind or support your decision, depending on the circumstances.

The other monitoring technique that will help you is a temperature and humidity gauge. This is readily available for under $50 at electronics stores and can help you determine how your building is responding to outside temperature and humidity conditions.

Using the information you have gained from the above steps, fix any performance problems your home may already have. This will not only reduce your current energy use but also improve your building's chances of being able to withstand climate change fluctuations for a longer time. With luck, this might keep your building functioning properly so that major remodeling to respond to climate shifts won't be necessary.

Air infiltration or leakage through wall cavities will carry more moisture into walls than diffusion through materials. In fact a one square inch hole in a piece of gypsum wallboard will allow about a quart of moisture a day to flow through the wall cavities in winter under normal types of conditions in a cold climate (Lstiburek). That's a lot of moisture that can come in contact with cold surfaces and condense inside the walls. The thermal imaging inspection discussed in the sidebar can help locate these and other points of moisture intrusion into the walls so they can be sealed.

The evaluation performed in the previous steps will also help determine if it is worth installing extra or missing insulation and if it is worth replacing recessed can-type light fixtures with airtight ones.

Once you have made the improvements, continue to monitor to see if the moisture conditions in your home are improving. It is not always possible to correct every problem cost effectively. In these situations careful monitoring and temporary first-aid measures during times of adverse conditions may be all that is necessary. If you find the moisture conditions are not improving then other excess moisture problems remain to be dealt with.

There are temporary measures you can use to sustain your home's durability when these adverse conditions develop. If you discover that certain times of the day or certain seasons present more of a moisture infiltration problem, you may be able to control it by using a portable dehumidifier to remove excess moisture. Or you may institute moisture reduction activities such as leaving the bathroom fan running longer to remove the extra moisture from your shower. You may find that temporary insulation panels for windows or insulated draperies may help keep surfaces from developing condensation, or you might need to keep furnishings pulled a little further away from walls to allow air exchange. You may need to keep closet or cabinet doors open to allow warm air circulation.

There are so many different possibilities that may vary dramatically based on the climate zone, but in general if it is cold outside, and you still find excess moisture is moving from the interior of the home into wall cavities, ceilings or floors and condensing there, you may want to reduce the amount of moisture in the indoor air and reduce the amount of air that can get into the walls.

If you find humid outdoor air is moving into your walls from the outside, you may want to slightly warm the walls to just above the dew point to prevent moisture condensation. Another helpful temporary technique is to slightly pressurize the interior of the home with dehumidified air to keep humid air from being able to flow into the home. A small fresh air return leading into a dehumidifier can usually accomplish this.

Some of the changes that may be necessary for buildings to respond to climate change can be expensive. Long-term measures to improve your home's ability to withstand adverse conditions should be carefully planned. Also consider what steps would be necessary to undo those measures if they turn out to be wrong. This is one area where some expert planning can help. For example, it is time to re-roof and you want to upgrade the roof's ability to withstand damage by covering the entire underlayment with a peel and stick membrane. Will this result in moisture being trapped in your attic space and condensing on the cold underside of the roof in winter? Might it be better for your geographical area to use peel and stick membranes only on the seams and use plywood panels which are better able to breathe than OSB for the underlayment?

Carefully consider any applications of moisture barriers. Since they don't breathe these can be helpful under some circumstances and disastrous in others. Before adding vinyl wallpaper, elastomeric paints or impermeable decorations such as glass-enclosed framed pictures to exterior walls, figure out if the moisture flow from warm to cold will become trapped behind the material. You may need to install spacers behind the picture frame to encourage air circulation. Vinyl wallpaper with microperforations is becoming available, but it still might not breathe enough to prevent problems. An alternative to wallpaper is faux painting using permeable latex or natural stains.

By using flexible measures that improve your home's ability to respond to extremes at both ends of the moisture flow spectrum you will be better able to adjust to temporary climate swings. A variable or double air conditioning system that can run for longer periods to dehumidify and then be turned up only when needed for extra cooling is an energy efficient and flexible way to control moisture. By understanding your building's moisture characteristics you will be better equipped to use simple steps like opening and closing windows or using ventilation fans with automatic humidistat controls set to come on when ventilation is needed. This again provides for flexibility.

There are times when immediate action makes sense, and other times when it pays to wait. Our present home has a wood shake roof that is 18 years old and nearing the end of its useful life, so it's time to decide the type of roofing system I will replace it with. This last summer we had 35 mile-per-hour winds gusting up to 50 miles-per-hour. Many of my neighbors sustained roof damage. We didn't, but it's now time to start thinking about replacing the roof with an upgrade that will be able to withstand even stronger winds. Our attic space is fully vented so I could use a full peel and stick membrane for covering the underlayment before the roof goes on. If I did not have a vented attic but, for example, an open-beam ceiling, then the full peel and stick membrane would be on the cold side of the roof and likely to trap and condense moisture in the winter. For that situation I could use an eight-inch peel and stick membrane only over the seam and a covering of roofing felt prior to the finish roof (shingles) being installed. This would provide better ability for the unvented roof to breathe and prevent condensation. This leads to the last point of continued monitoring.

For continued flexibility and to understand building conditions, continued monitoring is necessary. Most people take their car in for an oil change and checkup every 3,000 to 6,000 miles. Most homes don't fare as well. People have a home inspection completed prior to purchasing a house and that is it until the house is sold or develops problems. I would like to suggest a routine checkup every 15 months. This means it will be looked at in each of the different seasons once every five years. This is not the same type of inspection you would have done when purchasing a home, which is basically an inspection to identify what's broken. This would be a performance inspection to keep your home in tune and ready to protect you as best it can when extreme weather events occur.

What You Can Do

- Don't make any unnecessary changes until you understand the potential problems.

- Learn everything you can about your building and how it should function and respond to various climate events. A good resource for this is buildingscience.com.

- Determine the conditions that cause your building to take on moisture and those that cause it to lose moisture by measuring moisture levels and using WUFI simulations.

- Fix problems that adversely affect the performance of your home.

- Monitor to be sure the improvements you made actually do improve your home's performance and are not making things worse.

- Decide what temporary measures you will use to sustain your home's durability during adverse conditions.

- Determine what long-term measures you will use to improve your home's ability to withstand adverse conditions and what steps would be necessary to undo those measures if they turn out to be wrong.

- Try to use flexible measures that improve your home's ability to respond to extremes at both ends of the moisture flow spectrum.

- Decide when you will implement corrective measures.

- Continue monitoring, fine tuning and adjusting as necessary.

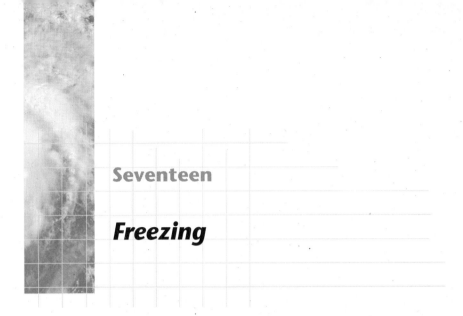

Seventeen

Freezing

Home is where the heart is.

— Pliny

Most of Canada and many parts of the northern United States, as well as areas at higher elevations, experience routine freezing. Buildings in these areas are constructed to withstand these conditions so collapsed roofs, frozen plumbing pipes, ice dams and heaving founda-

tions are uncommon. When they do occur it is usually because the heat went off while the building was temporarily unoccupied or some condition was changed. For example, insulation may have been pushed away and not replaced. When freezing conditions result in water entering a building, it is much easier to repair and dry than when a building becomes flooded from ground or surface water. Melting ice and snow, as well as water from burst frozen plumbing pipes is generally considered clean water. This means that as well as the structure itself, many more personal contents

This traditional steep thatched roof in England sheds snow and water before they can penetrate the interior.

141

and furnishings can be salvaged, provided the water is discovered promptly and professional emergency restorative drying is begun within 24 to 48 hours. If snow or ice enters because of a collapsed roof, parts of the building may be weakened and ready to collapse, so this is definitely a job for professionals. If the snow and ice can be removed while they are still frozen, so much the better; the amount of drying necessary will be greatly reduced since the water hasn't soaked into materials.

Climate Change Effects

Climate change trends have been toward warming, however short-term weather has demonstrated extreme swings. Even though the climate is warming, communities are experiencing unexpected snow and cold snaps. Snow and ice are generally not a big problem when buildings are constructed for these conditions. Roofs are usually designed to hold the weight of snow that is historically expected to accumulate, but unexpected heavy snowfall in areas not accustomed to it may overtax the design leading to collapse. If your home is located in an area that doesn't typically experience high levels of snow, you can help prevent damage by being prepared to deal with unexpected snow accumulation.

A roof cricket helps divert snow to prevent it from building up or damaging the chimney. This cricket was too small to prevent roof damage and water entering the building.

Roofs and Freezing Weather

Hip or gable roofs with a slope greater than 3.5 are generally the best for dealing with snow. The less the slope of the roof, the less chance the snow will slide off and clear itself before overloading. Fancy roofs with valleys or other intricate features are more likely to accumulate more snow on portions of the roof. Even if you have a steep slope to your roof, ice storms can cause ice to form directly on the roofing materials. Ice is much heavier than snow. Once ice has formed on a roof, any snow that lands on top is less likely to slough off by itself.

A minimum typical roof load capacity would be about 20-pounds-per-square-foot, although most roofs can carry more. Without knowledge of your roof's load capacity, it's best to play it safe. According to the University of Minnesota, "A one-inch layer of water or ice weighs approximately five pounds-per-square-foot. So a roof designed for a 20-pounds-per-square-foot snow load could theoretically hold up to four inches of ice. How much snow is that? Meteorologists often estimate that about 12 inches of snow is equivalent to one inch of water. Using that 'rule of thumb,' a roof should hold up to four feet of snow. Wet and packed snow weigh more per inch of depth, meaning that a roof may only be able to hold up to three feet of snow " (Jacobson). A roof that has been damaged by insects or is otherwise defective may hold even less. If you suspect your roof is overloaded, evacuate the building. The roof needs to be cleared of snow well before it reaches the overload point. Being on or under an overloaded roof may be deadly if it collapses.

Don't use a shovel or metal edge to rake the roof. It may damage the roof materials. Use a specially designed snow roof rake. This should be done from the ground, or hire a professional who can use the appro-

These palm trees have been wrapped during winter to help protect them from damage during unseasonably cold, windy weather.

priate tie-offs and safety gear. Getting on a snow- or ice-covered roof is dangerous and may lead to even more roof damage since cold roof materials can be very brittle. It is best if the snow is removed while it is still freshly fallen or just melting. Don't wait until it starts to refreeze — chipping the ice away can also damage the roof.

Another caution while raking the snow off the roof, especially if it is starting to melt, is the possibility of a mini-avalanche. As the snow begins to melt the water will begin running down the roof under the snow, loosening the material so the entire bank of snow may slide off at once. If you are standing on the ground using a snow roof rake make sure to stand back far enough that the snow won't dump on your head. If the weight is enough to worry about it causing the structure to collapse, it is more than enough to seriously injure you. One way to stay out of the dump zone is to use extension poles manufactured to fit the roof snow rake. That way you can stand back far enough that any falling snow will miss you.

Flat roofs can be a huge problem since there is no easy way to get the snow or ice off the roof. More than four inches of ice or undrained water on a flat roof could be enough to cause the roof to collapse.

Foundation Heaving Due to Freeze/Thaw

Damage from foundation heaving due to freeze/thaw conditions occurs when the water in the soil expands as it freezes. Foundations that have their footings in the areas that freeze and thaw will be moved by the expansion and contraction of the water. This is the reason that foundation footings constructed in areas of the country that have soil freeze in the winter need to be much deeper than other parts of the country. The support footing for the building needs to extend below any layer that might freeze. With the planet warming, it is likely that most existing foundation depths will be adequate to prevent heaving. However if climate change should result in soil freezing in areas where this normally doesn't occur, then major problems with shallow foundations heaving are likely to occur. These problems would require professional engineering solutions, but temporary measures could potentially forestall damage by heating the foundation basement or crawlspace to prevent the water from freezing and expanding. A well-drained soil will be less likely to freeze under these conditions. Another condition involving freezing soil, called adfreezing, may occur and cause frost heaving damage even if the footing is well below the layer of soil that freezes.

According to information published by the National Research Council of Canada: "Movements in the soil resulting from ice lens growth can be transmitted to the structure if soil freezes to the foundation walls or supporting columns" (Penner). An ice lens is a type of ice crystal formation shaped very much like the lens of a camera. This is a much more common problem for structures with shallow foundations such as garages, carports and unheated buildings. When adfreezing occurs the soil freezes to the sides of the foundation. This usually starts at the surface and moves downward as conditions get colder. As the ice freezes to the sides of the foundation it applies an upward lifting force. When the upward force exceeds the weight of the structure, it lifts the house. Adfreezing occurs at shallow depths and can potentially develop with buildings that are subject to freezing soil conditions near the surface from short-term extreme weather swings. In order for the foundation to be pushed upwards the soil under the foundation must be susceptible to frost heaving. Adfreezing is most common in soils that are subject to seasonal frost. It is likely that different areas of soil under the home will freeze at different rates and some areas of soil around the foundation may not freeze at all. This causes the foundation to move in different ways at different points causing the building to be torn in different directions.

The foundation damage can get worse each year as the adfreezing lifts a building foundation through the soil. If soil falls into the space formed by the uplifting of the foundation the building can't sink back to the original level. Each year damages become progressively worse.

There are ways of constructing buildings to protect the foundations from adfreezing. The simplest way is to make sure the foundation is well drained using a gravel bed surrounding the foundation. All parts of the foundation should be well drained anyway, but there are many ways to accomplish the drainage. By using the gravel bed method the drainage will keep moisture away from the foundation; it will also help prevent the adfreezing. It is important the gravel bed be well drained to prevent ponding water from freezing and defeating the purpose of the gravel (Penner).

Prevention in Existing Buildings

A method for helping to minimize damage from adfreezing in existing structures with raised foundations involves digging around the foundation and installing water-impermeable rigid insulation along the outside of the foundation walls to a depth below the expected frost level. Insulating the perimeter foundation can help to keep the foundation heat from escaping from under the home. By installing the insulation, a percentage of the heat from the home keeps the surface between the foundation and insulation warmer so the water can't freeze to the foundation. Homes in areas with adfreezing need to be kept warm. Shutting off the heat in these buildings for a vacation during the winter or in a vacant summer home could result in the building shifting on its foundation.

Other engineered methods include anchoring the building to the earth with tie-downs. As a temporary measure professionals have injected lubricants or applied them to the foundation to help prevent the freezing layer from adhering to the foundation. This method is only effective for a few years before requiring reapplication (Penner).

Adfreezing is relatively rare in buildings with heated basements or cellars providing the interior walls are not well-insulated. This provides a strategy for preventing damage if climate change results in frost occasionally forming in the soil. If the basement or cellar isn't heated when adfreezing conditions develop, you may need to add some temporary heat to the substructure. Make sure the heat is evenly distributed throughout the substructure so that you don't end up with parts of the house heaving. If the foundation is insulated on the interior side of perimeter walls, the heat may not be able to penetrate to prevent the heaving from occurring. Using extra heat to save the foundation will cost extra on your energy bill, and is certainly not a preferred method, but it can buy you a little time until an engineered solution can be developed.

What You Can Do

- When building or purchasing a home look for a roof with a slope greater than 3.5. The greater the slope the less likely snow or ice will accumulate.

- Know your roof's load capacity and don't exceed the load limit for snow or ice. If you live in an area not typically associated with snowfall

Rigid insulation panels can help prevent energy loss from the basement and potential adfreezing.

assume your roof can hold no more than four inches of ice (assume one foot of snow is approximately equal to one inch of ice).

- Keep your foundation well drained to prevent adfreezing.

- If you are in an area not typically associated with soil freezing, consider warming the substructure to keep ice from fusing with the foundation resulting in adfreeze damage.

- Excavate and insulate the outside of the foundation to a depth below the expected freeze level.

- Use coarse gravel or rock with drainage as backfill to prevent adfreezing when constructing new foundations. If your foundation ever requires major repairs, this may be a good time to add additional drainage and backfill with gravel to help reduce future problems.

Eighteen

Ice Damming

In the fields of observation, chance favors only the prepared mind.

— Louis Pasteur

Ice damming occurs when snow repeatedly melts and refreezes before it can drain from the roof.

NOAA HISTORIC NWS COLLECTION

Ice dams form when snow that has landed on a warm part of a roof melts and runs off into a cold frozen area of the roof or when a short-term warming trend begins melting snow. As the water encounters a colder surface roof area it refreezes. One of the more common places for this to occur is along the roof's eave overhang. A barrier of ice forms becoming larger until the melted snow runoff fills the area behind the ice dam. As the liquid water accumulates in this warmer area of the roof it seeps under the roofing material instead of draining. Once the water has penetrated the roofing material it continues to flow laterally and vertically downward along the path of least resistance. Frequently the water flows into the building. This area is often just above where the building's walls are located. The trapped melted snow water runs down into the perimeter wall cavities of the house. The wet insulation in the walls no longer properly functions, which

149

Can-type lighting and other heat sources in the attic can increase the likelihood of ice dams developing.

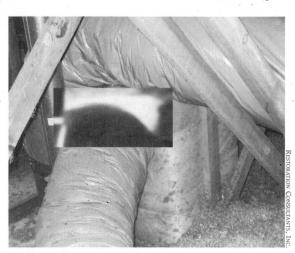

Leaky ductwork not only wastes energy but increases the likelihood of icedams. An infrared camera was used to easily identify this area of heat loss.

may result in the water freezing inside the insulation and the wall cavities. In this case the wall cavities may remain frozen until the weather warms up enough to thaw and create water damage.

Climate Change Effects

A study of the causes of ice damming in existing structures leads to an understanding of how ice damming problems could easily develop in buildings exposed to extreme weather events. This is because homes in areas with moderate climates will frequently have multiple conditions that can result in ice damming. If extreme weather results in snow where it is unusual, the homes are more likely to suffer from ice dam-related damage.

Conditions Leading to Ice Dams

Missing insulation from an attic space is a common situation that leads to ice damming. The heat from the warm interior of the house radiates upward through the uninsulated ceiling and warms the underside of the roof. This warming causes the snow on the roof to melt and run down the roof slope, channeling under the remaining snow, until it drains from the roof or reaches an area that is cold enough for the water to refreeze into ice. Buildings constructed in areas that historically have freezing weather and snow are usually built to avoid warm spots developing on the roof; however, during construction the insulation in the attic may be left uneven or with gaps. Insulation may also be scooped away during maintenance activities or compressed when it is walked on without replacing the material.

Heat sources in the attic may also result in the formation of ice dams. It is common to find uninsulated recessed can lights, furnace systems, leaky ductwork and missing insulation in building attics. If these heat sources are present in attics in buildings that experience snow, the heat may transfer through the roofing materials and melt the snow.

Most attic spaces are ventilated to help prevent excessive heat buildup in the summer and moisture condensation in the winter. In climates that don't experience freezing temperatures attic insulation is frequently not installed all the way to the eaves since the insulation can block the air-flow ventilating the attic. The ventilation is important in unconditioned attics to prevent the formation of condensation. The eave vents typically will have about 18 inches of insulation left out to provide the ventilation. This is a prime location for ice damming to occur since the heat from the room below warms the attic.

Typically recessed can lights are not insulted or airtight. Insulation must be kept back away from them usually at least three inches from all sides for cooling so the heat coming off them doesn't cause a fire. The uninsulated space and the heat from the can light will warm the attic. If enough lights are present, the excess heat may be enough to melt snow resulting in ice damming. The installation of furnace systems and leaky ductwork in attic spaces may also contribute enough heat to result in ice damming for similar reasons.

This thermal image demonstrates missing insulation.

Preventing Ice Damming

Diagnosing conditions that lead to ice damming is similar to the techniques used for energy conservation evaluations for heat loss. One of the most effective techniques utilizes thermal imaging cameras to look for hot spots on roofs and

RESTORATION CONSULTANTS, INC.

missing or compromised insulation in the attic. There are companies that offer thermal image scans for energy conservation purposes throughout North America. Many public utilities can offer a referral for these services. This is one of the most effective methods for diagnosing and preventing ice damming with the added benefit of determining how to reduce energy costs at the same time.

If you find yourself in a situation where ice dams are likely to form, you can limit or prevent the damage by taking appropriate action at the right time. If your roof has hot spots that will lead to melting and refreezing you will need to remove the snow from the drainage path. This should be from where the hot spots are located all the way to the edge of the roof. It is important to remove the snow while it is still fresh before it has a chance to thaw and refreeze. This requires some care so as not to damage the roof or yourself. (See Chapter 17: Freezing.)

If water has already refrozen on the roof, chipping the ice away is likely to create roof damage. Create a couple of grooves in the ice to allow the ponding water to drain off. These grooves should not penetrate to the roof materials or additional damage will occur. Most hardware stores in parts of the country that have ice and snow sell heat strips that can be used to melt the ice. Melt it so the water created can drain instead of filling the area behind the dam. This work is very dangerous; it is much better if these problems can be avoided by removing the snow before it becomes ice or making sure the roof doesn't have warm patches likely to lead to ice damming. One major difficulty is that hardware stores stock what they can sell. If you begin experiencing ice damming in an area that has not previously been prone

This oversized truss shows insulation that is blocked or dammed at the eave with a soffit dam (a piece of fiberglass batt or rigid insulation). A rafter baffle creates a channel for air flow.

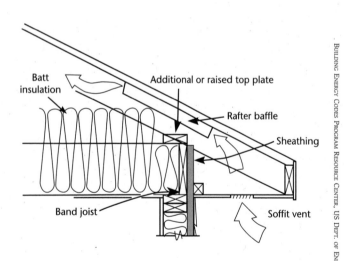

Batt insulation

Additional or raised top plate

Rafter baffle

Sheathing

Band joist

Soffit vent

BUILDING ENERGY CODES PROGRAM RESOURCE CENTER, US DEPT. OF ENERGY

to ice formation, the tools for solving the problems may not be immediately available.

If ice damming has already resulted in water damage to your home, you have only a limited period to get it dry before mold growth occurs. Treat this as emergency water damage from clean water flooding (see Chapter 8: Flooding for more on clean water flood damage). If ice damming has resulted in water damage that isn't discovered right away, mold remediation may be required. Take precautions to prevent the mold spores from spreading to other parts of your home. You may be able to avoid or limit mold growth if you hire a professional water damage restoration company immediately.

What You Can Do

- Replace missing insulation. Keeping the attic floor well-insulated will minimize the amount of heat that rises through the attic from the house.

- Use ventilation baffles at the eaves so that the attic can have ventilation but insulation can be brought right up to the eave instead of having to leave a space.

- Install airtight insulation contact (ATIC) rated can lights and bring the insulation right up to them as well. Don't do this with regular can lights or you might have a fire.

- Seal furnace systems and ductwork to prevent energy loss into the unconditioned attic space. A thermal imaging scan will reveal where heat loss is occurring from ductwork. A Duct Blaster or Blower Door test can tell how much energy is being lost and to what degree it has been corrected.

- Make sure your clothes dryer is vented to the outside and not into the attic. If the dryer vent penetrates through the roof, it may get hot enough to cause localized ice damming in the middle of the roof instead of the more common ice dam that forms at the edge of the roof.

- Don't install hot water heaters or heating systems in the attic.
- Keep the attic well ventilated. The colder the attic space is kept, the less melting and refreezing will lead to ice dams on the roof.
- When you re-roof, plan on having a water-repellent shingle underlayment membrane installed under your roof covering to a point beyond where pooling water from ice dams may accumulate.
- Not only can the proactive steps outlined here help prevent major damage from ice damming, but they will save you dollars on your energy bill and correspondingly reduce the emission of greenhouse gases leading to global warming in the first place.

Nineteen

Frozen Plumbing

The greatest antidote to worry, whether you're getting ready for spaceflight or facing a problem of daily life, is preparation ... the more you try to envision what might happen and what your best response and options are, the more you are able to allay your fears about the future.

— Senator John Glenn

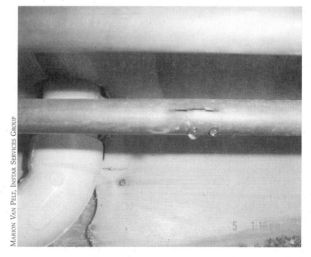

Freezing water may expand and rupture plumbing pipes.

Frozen pipes don't actually rupture because of expanding ice increasing the circumference of the pipe, as is commonly believed. Instead the bursting of metal pipes is caused by increasing pressure from liquid water. In his book *Water in Buildings: An Architect's Guide to Moisture and Mold,* William B. Rose explains the mechanism more thoroughly. He credits the research presented in a Master's thesis at the University of Alaska in Fairbanks under the direction of John Zarling, where the student made pressure measurements of pipes subject to bursting. As the temperature of the metal pipe drops below freezing, the water

MARION VAN PELT, INSTAR SERVICES GROUP

155

begins to freeze on the walls of the pipe until that portion of the pipe is blocked with ice. If you were to turn on the spigot after that plug formed, and leave it open, no water would flow but the pipe would not rupture no matter how solidly frozen it became. If the spigot is left closed the ice continues to freeze and expand along the length of the pipe toward the fixture. This causes the pressure in the remaining water in the pipe to increase dramatically. It is the pressure being exerted on the liquid water remaining in the pipe as the ice expands that will finally cause the pipe to burst. "Of course, under high pressure the system will fail at its weakest point. If it fails at the pipe, it is likely to fail at the point where the pipe is least ductile (at least in metal pipe), and that is at the coldest point where the ice meets the water. This is what creates the illusion that it is ice that ruptures the pipe" (Rose). This understanding of how frozen pipes burst will help you understand how to prevent plumbing from bursting if you unexpectedly experience a cold snap in your community — leave the spigot open to drip and release the pressure from the expanding ice.

Climate Change Effects

Climate change results in temperature swings. Parts of the country that don't typically freeze may suddenly be plunged into short-term freeze conditions. In the early spring of 2007, southern California and Florida experienced extreme fluctuations in temperature that resulted in freezing conditions. News reports focused on the agricultural damage to the citrus industry, but many homeowners woke up with frozen plumbing. Water damage restoration contractors were kept busy cleaning up after the flooding that occurred from burst pipes.

Regional building codes usually dictate how deeply water supply lines must be buried below the historical freeze/thaw line. Erratic weather patterns may result in snap freezes in some areas that don't traditionally freeze. Other areas that do freeze may have even colder temperatures. The permanent fix is to dig the pipes deeper, but that is expensive. If you have the plumbing line's path located in the ground, you may be able to cover the surface with a deep layer of mulch to help prevent the soil underneath from freezing to the level of the pipes. If an area of pipe has frozen over once there is a good chance it will happen again. To prevent a reoccurrence add heat and insulation or shut off and drain the plumbing when the temperature plummets. Of course if you have to drain the plumbing you won't have water, but shutting off and draining during cold snaps is better than bursting a pipe.

Frozen pipes are usually discovered first thing in the morning, when water is first used. If none of the taps provide water under pressure then the freeze point is located before it enters the structure. If only certain taps don't work the frozen pipe is located in some section of the distribution line.

First-Aid for Frozen Plumbing

As soon as you discover your pipes are freezing you should take action by immediately opening all the hot and cold water taps just a bit to let the water drip. The open valve will help keep the pipes from freezing solid and release the pressure that usually causes the pipes to burst. The most important taps to leave slightly open are the ones at the furthest end and highest elevation of the run of pipes. This way a flow of water will help prevent freezing along the entire length of your plumbing. Be aware that many communities have an inadequate water supply. If everyone were to run excessive amounts of their water simultaneously, there might not be enough for the community. You may want to collect the dripping water so as not to waste it and to have it available if the water supply does shut down.

If there is even the smallest trickle of water coming past the freeze point it should be encouraged by leaving the tap open. Even if water isn't flowing, the open tap may be able to release the pressure of expansion that usually bursts pipes. The water that is coming from the main or the well may be cold, but it will still be warmer than the frozen water in the pipes and will help to defrost the pipes and prevent the buildup of pressure as the ice expands. Once you get the water flowing leave it running at a trickle from any spigot that you are concerned may refreeze until the cold snap has passed. This is especially important for water lines supplying exterior spigots or plumbing lines in exterior walls.

If pipes inside your home have frozen solidly without spigots being opened in time to release pressure, there is a good chance the expanding water has caused them to burst. Sometimes the expansion will cause a split that will run along the length of the pipe. Other times the expanding ice will cause the pipe to separate at a joint. Don't stop looking after you find the first break — there may be more. If you can't stay around to monitor the plumbing closely for breaks, shut off the water at the main supply to the home or you may come home to a flood that begins as soon as the pipe defrosts.

To defrost frozen pipes, open the tap slightly and gently heat the pipe from the end towards the blockage. Use a blow dryer or heat gun, not an open flame.

If the water supply line leading to the house bursts you will most likely learn this only after it thaws and the water starts to flow. You may also be able to determine if there is a burst pipe with a hidden flow if your water meter indicates water use when the taps are all off, or your well pump is running but reduced water is being delivered An outdoor pipe that bursts may be flowing underground and wasting lots of water, but it shouldn't cause damage to the inside of your home if there is good drainage. If the pipe breaks in a slab or inaccessible area you will probably need to shut the water off to the house and call for professional leak detection assistance.

If a certain part of your household plumbing freezes, a water shut-off valve that allows you to drain that section of plumbing to prevent it from freezing but still allows you to have water in other parts of your home may temporarily solve the problem. You may also be able to wrap the offending section of plumbing with electrical heat tape that can be plugged in to heat the pipes. Long-term fixes may include adding additional insulation, or rerouting plumbing lines to prevent future freezing.

You may be able to defrost frozen pipes using a blow dryer or electrical heating tape. Make sure any electrical equipment is plugged into a ground fault interrupter to prevent electrocution if water unexpectedly begins to flow from the break. Start before the blockage and work towards the middle. Don't use an open flame or blow torch due to the risk of fire and melting solder joints or plastic pipes. Once water flow has been restored watch closely for drips from joints or gushing water.

If burst pipes have resulted in water damage to the building you have only a limited period to get it dry before mold growth occurs. Treat this as emergency freshwater damage.

If hidden water damage from burst pipes results in mold growth, or isn't discovered right away, take precautions to prevent the mold from spreading and get it remediated.

If you will be away for an extended period you may decide to protect the plumbing by winterizing the home. This involves draining the plumbing, which requires opening the taps with the highest and lowest elevations. Blowing the water out of the plumbing lines may be a good idea since any residual water trapped in a segment of plumbing may also freeze. Do not turn off or drain the hot water heater for short absences or unless you have to because of a broken pipe. The heat from the hot water heater will frequently travel by conduction through the hot water pipes for a distance which may help keep pipes from freezing. Most hot water heaters will have a shut-off valve at the unit. Once that valve is off the hot water plumbing lines can be drained while the hot water heater remains filled and on.

What You Can Do

- Insulate pipes that are exposed and add more insulation to walls, attics and other areas where pipes are located.

- Use caulking to seal cracks and other openings in the foundation and exterior walls. If air leaks exist, subfreezing air flowing through them will freeze plumbing pipes faster than if the insulation were missing from around the pipes. Even if pipes are insulated, air leaks can still cause them to freeze.

- Leave bathroom and kitchen cabinet doors open to allow heat to circulate around the plumbing, especially if they are located on an outside wall.

- Let the water run at a slow trickle if a cold snap threatens to freeze plumbing, or drain the water system, especially if your house will be unattended during cold periods.

- The sprinkler system should be drained and disconnected.

- Garden hoses should be disconnected.

- Place mulch over shallow water/drain lines.

- Shut off and drain water lines that can't be protected.

- Consider installing a water monitor to automatically shut the water off and limit the amount of water released if a pipe should burst.

- If pipes freeze solidly don't use an open flame to defrost them. Electrical heat tape, a heat lamp or other gentle methods of defrosting the plumbing is much safer, as long as electrical equipment is plugged into a GFI.

- Watch carefully for burst areas as the pipes are defrosted. It may be the pipe has burst but you can't tell by inspecting it until the water begins to flow.

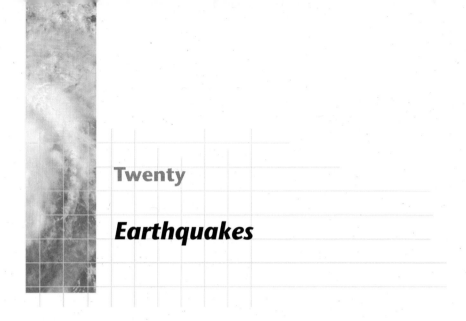

Twenty

Earthquakes

So convenient a thing it is to be a reasonable creature, since it enables one to find or make a reason for everything one has a mind to do.

— Benjamin Franklin

As I began my research for this book I knew I had a firm basis for my premise that climate change would lead to greater problems for our buildings and that preventative measures could in many cases reduce or eliminate the damage. Damage from hurricanes, tornados, hail and lightning were already apparent and published scientific evidence indicates increasing occurrences. Other issues, like the shifting of homes built on expansive clay or trapped water vapor from increasing humidity, develop more slowly and are difficult to observe unless looked for. However, it is still easy to understand how climate change could lead to an increase in their occurrence. The thought that global warming could lead to earthquakes, tsunamis and volcanic eruptions initially seemed far-fetched. Yet according to researchers, melting glaciers appear to be increasing the incidence of earthquakes. In an article published in *Science*, Göran Ekström and Victor C. Tsai from Harvard University and Meredith Nettles from

Columbia University reported that the incidence of "glacial earthquakes" is increasing, especially in summer months when the glacial ice melts faster. The loss of compression as glaciers shift unexpectedly has resulted in a doubling of seismic movements up to 5.1 on the Richter scale (Ekström).

Protecting your home from earthquakes involves securing it in much the same way that it needs to be secured from high winds. Additional information on surviving an earthquake can be obtained from FEMA and the Red Cross at fema.gov/hazard/earthquake/eq_before. Further information has been produced by the US Geological Survey: "Putting Down Roots in Earthquake Country," at pubs.usgs.gov/gip/2005/15.

Time will tell what other types of interactions may be occurring. Large chunks of ice dropping into the ocean from glaciers may result in tsunamis. I've yet to see compelling evidence that climate change is having an influence on volcanic activity; however, volcanic activity can certainly result in climate change by belching huge quantities of greenhouse gases into the atmosphere.

Part Three
Building for Resiliency

The preceding chapters have explained how climate change may adversely affect our homes and buildings. The chapters in this section explain how structural methods and materials can be integrated in home design for resilient modern construction that will be flexible and durable, especially when faced with interacting conditions involving extreme wind, water and freezing. This section explains how roof, wall, foundation and site all affect one another, requiring buildings to be constructed as integrated, whole systems to function properly and recover quickly from extreme weather conditions.

Twenty-One

The Building Site

There are many reasons that people choose to live in various areas. They may choose a location to be close to family, friends, work, school, the ocean, the mountains, or have any number of other reasons. The building site is also a very important consideration. There is no place on our planet that doesn't have some risks associated with either location or site. Some of the risks are natural; others are man-made, and we are now beginning to be faced with a whole new range of risks that are the natural consequences of man-made climate change. It is not so common for people to decide where to build based on the risk of calamity although that may be starting to change. Some risks can be controlled and limited, others are perceived as being "worth the risk," but sometimes circumstances force a change in location. To a large extent the government will need to be involved in making major decisions regarding the continued habitability of some of our coastlines. Some highly populated areas will likely be "worth" the investment in building and maintaining levees for keeping water away from buildings. As these communities develop there must be a recognition that the location is at a higher risk. Each person needs to make personal decisions regarding these potential effects from climate change. Is it worth staying and implementing the necessary safeguards? Does moving or avoiding

"One way of increasing adaptive capacity is by introducing the consideration of climate change impacts in development planning, for example, by: including adaptation measures in land-use planning and infrastructure design."

(IPCC 2007 page 19 Summary for Policymakers)

the area make more sense? When should the move occur?

The Ideal Site

The ideal building site would be able to be well drained. The soil should be stable and not subject to movement. The soil shouldn't have radon or other harmful gases being emitted from underground. The location should be away from areas that are subject to extreme weather events. It may not always be possible to find such a location, but many problems such as freezing, expansive clay soils, lightning, hail and trapped moisture can be overcome with the proper construction techniques for the foundation walls and roof.

In order to be well drained the site should be well above the Base Flood Elevation (BFE) with an available gravity drainage path leading from the property to carry large amounts of water away. The site should also be located so that water from neighboring properties doesn't need to drain through your property. Determining the BFE for your property has been described in Chapter 8. This information can also be used to determine the availability and costs for flood insurance.

Radon

Radon is a radioactive decomposition product of uranium in the soil. Radon gas is a naturally occurring indoor air pollutant that enters homes built over underground deposits of uranium. Uranium in the soil under the home breaks down into other radioactive compounds which eventually become radium and then radon gas. The half-life of radon is 3.8 days. If the radon gas is close enough to the surface of the soil it can percolate upward and be released from the earth before it decays back to a solid form, allowing the radioactive gas to rise up and collect inside a home sitting on top.

If your home hasn't already been built, radon reduction strategies are easy to implement for the well-drained site since the foundation drainage system can also double for radon reduction. The soil can be evaluated prior to construction for radon gas but it is difficult to predict what type of radon level will be present in a building after it has been constructed. Climate change can result in cracks forming in foundations due to the movement of expansive clay soils. These cracks then become

The US EPA states that all homes should be tested for radon, which can occur in any zone.

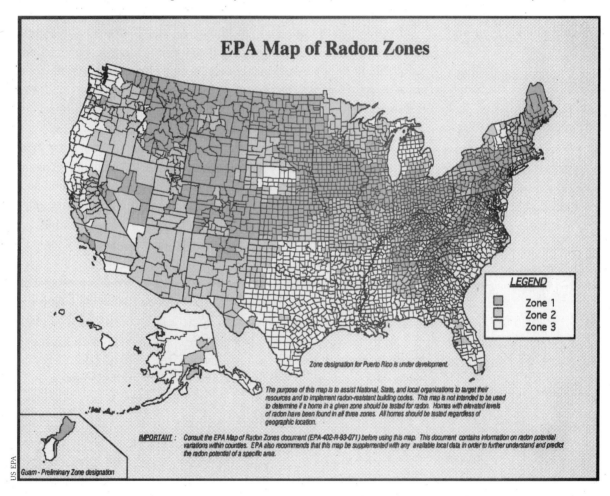

EPA Map of Radon Zones

LEGEND
Zone 1
Zone 2
Zone 3

Zone designation for Puerto Rico is under development.

The purpose of this map is to assist National, State, and local organizations to target their resources and to implement radon-resistant building codes. This map is not intended to be used to determine if a home in a given zone should be tested for radon. Homes with elevated levels of radon have been found in all three zones. All homes should be tested regardless of geographic location.

IMPORTANT : Consult the EPA Map of Radon Zones document (EPA-402-R-93-071) before using this map. This document contains information on radon potential variations within counties. EPA also recommends that this map be supplemented with any available local data in order to further understand and predict the radon potential of a specific area.

US EPA

Guam - Preliminary Zone designation

direct pathways for the radon to enter your home. Buildings constructed on expansive soil may also be more likely to develop radon problems as they get older and foundation cracks form. Radon problems that develop in buildings can usually be corrected. Most radon repairs cost a few hundred dollars or even less if the structure was built to avoid problems with expansive soils and has good drainage. It would be rare for a radon problem to require extensive repairs costing more than a couple of thousand dollars for a single family home.

If you've never evaluated your home for radon gas, now is a good time to do it. The US EPA recommends that every home be evaluated for radon (US EPA). This can usually be performed by using a simple do-it-yourself charcoal canister test that will cost you less than $25. The canister is exposed according to directions then sent to the laboratory for analysis.

If levels are less than 1.0 picocurie you are doing about as good as is reasonably practical. At 4.0 picocuries — the level at which the EPA recommends you definitely take action — the measurement typically will take about 48 hours.

A level of 4.0 picocuries of radon per liter of air translates into an increased risk of lung cancer approximately equivalent to smoking half a pack of cigarettes a day.

If necessary, there are some relatively low-cost methods for reducing radon levels. Some of these will also help reduce the amount of water vapor coming from the soil into your home at the same time. If you find that your basement is likely to be having moisture problems, or you intend to make changes to the basement's drainage, it makes sense to use a system that will reduce radon and moisture at the same time.

Twenty-Two

The Foundation

The foundation is the base of the home. The clichés you have heard about building on a strong foundation, or building from the foundation up are rules for life that use construction examples as metaphors. Mistakes in design or construction sometimes don't show up until after the building is exposed to extreme weather conditions such as flooding. Although this is true for all parts of a home, it can be especially true regarding foundations. It's a cliché, but true, that you must build on a strong foundation.

Water-related problems can seriously weaken foundations. Water can pass through a foundation in a couple of different ways. One way is when liquid water is drawn through by capillary or osmotic action. When water flows through masonry it will dissolve salts and carry them to the surface where they deposit. These salt deposits are called efflorescence. Foundations should be drained so they do not have capillary action. The other is when water passes through the concrete as water vapor. Even when properly constructed, some water vapor will still pass through foundations. Most flooring manufacturers allow up to 3 pounds of moisture to pass through a slab foundation every 24 hours for each 1,000 square feet of floor surface. This means a 2,000-square-foot home with a concrete slab should be able to handle approximately 3 quarts of water coming into the indoor environment every day from the slab. When the levels get higher, many types of flooring begin to fail.

Other types of foundations including basements can also have severe water problems when the foundation is installed in a way that allows water to pool near the foundation instead of being drained away. Flooded basements and crawlspaces can cause major damage to the supporting structure if not properly drained.

The Ideal Foundation

The ideal foundation must be well drained. Liquid water expands and contracts as it freezes; well-drained foundations avoid these tremendous hydrostatic forces. The well-drained basement foundation will also not run the risk of floating the building upward since the surrounding soils will not be able to fill with groundwater. Of course this means the well-drained foundation must be sited so that it remains completely above flood levels.

Pooled water can become water vapor that can migrate and penetrate the foundation. It is important to keep the foundation well drained to minimize not only liquid penetration, but water vapor as well. In addition to being protected from liquid water the ideal foundation will be able to accommodate the residual movement of water vapor through the foundation walls so that moisture will not be trapped. In addition to flowing from higher areas of concentration, water vapor also flows from hot to cold. Our basements will almost always be warmer than the soils that surround them, so the vapor flow will be from the basement outward into the soil. When these two principles compete, higher concentration to lower concentration will win over hot to cold. What actually happens is that equilibrium is reached based on the competition between these forces, but under almost every circumstance year-round water vapor will tend to dry toward the interior of the basement so again we need to keep as much moisture excluded as possible using a well-drained foundation with a vapor barrier on the outside of the foundation.

Deterioration of Iron Rebar

During my trip to England I visited various castle ruins that were being restored, one of which was the Glastonbury Abbey. During the 1980s this site underwent a restoration to repair some of the centuries of deterioration. Joints between the stones were cleaned of debris and deteriorated mortar. Iron rebar was added for reinforcing followed by grouting the joints with new mortar. In the last 25 years electrolysis has caused the rebar to degrade. As rebar corrodes it expands and causes fractures in the mortar. The restoration now has to be repeated to remove the iron rebar and replace it with non-corroding reinforcement.

This same sort of deterioration frequently occurs in foundations that have been reinforced using iron rebar. The iron adequately supports the foundation for a couple of decades but then weakens, resulting in cracking and separation when soils expand and contact or freeze/thaw occurs. As long as the soils supporting the foundation remain stable there is no problem, but as climate change results in changes in soil moisture and movement it is more likely for damage to occur to the foundation reinforced with iron rebar than with fiberglass rebar.

Fiberglass rebar is available by special order. It requires special pre-molded angle pieces since the fiberglass isn't able to be bent on the job-site. Many commercial projects, bridges, overpasses and parking structures are now being built using fiberglass rebar because of the added safety and longevity.

Restoration work on Glastonbury Abbey was performed using iron rebar about 30 years ago. The iron rebar is now being removed because of deterioration due to electrolysis.

The ideal foundation will not be located in an area where expansive soils are a risk. Since up to 50 percent of the soils in the US and some of the more populated border areas of Alberta, Saskatchewan and Manitoba have some expansive capabilities it is often necessary to build over such soils. In these cases the soil moisture content needs to be kept relatively constant and the soil stabilized by permanent treatment or the foundation engineered so that the expansive characteristics will not adversely affect the home. Iron rebar used to reinforce the foundation is subject to deterioration from electrolysis so fiberglass rebar is recommended to avoid this.

Types of Foundations
Slab-on-grade Foundations

Some parts of the country almost exclusively use slab-on-grade construction. This is especially common in areas with a high water table or where the soil does not freeze. They are one of the least expensive and easiest foundations to construct. The building is built on top of a cement slab poured on the earth, but there is a lot more to slab-on-grade foundations than just cement sitting on the top of the soil. The center part of the slab is typically much thinner than around the edges. The edges or perimeter go much deeper for two reasons. The first reason is to support the weight of the perimeter walls, which will all be load bearing. Secondly, the footing or base of the perimeter for the slab extends below the freeze/thaw point. This is true for all types of foundations. They must typically extend below the level of soil that will freeze. Slab foundations are rarely found in areas where the soil freezes since they must have a deep footer around the perimeter that extends below the freeze line. As long as such a deep footer must be installed, it makes sense to have a raised foundation.

The concrete that is used to form the slab is very porous and will allow both liquid water as well as water vapor to penetrate. One major concern for slab-on-grade foundations with climate change is that slabs

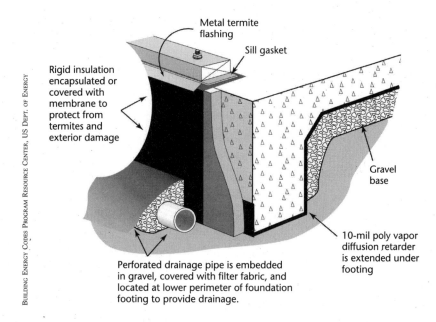

Metal termite flashing

Sill gasket

Rigid insulation encapsulated or covered with membrane to protect from termites and exterior damage

Gravel base

10-mil poly vapor diffusion retarder is extended under footing

Perforated drainage pipe is embedded in gravel, covered with filter fabric, and located at lower perimeter of foundation footing to provide drainage.

A well-drained foundation with a polyethylene layer properly installed can help prevent the flow of both liquid water and water vapor.

built in parts of the country where the soil is typically dry may have been built without an adequate vapor barrier, capillary break or drainage.

Raised Foundations

Crawlspaces are generally found under raised foundations, and are usually confined, with varying degrees of access. Homes built in parts of the country that freeze generally must have a foundation that extends below the soil freeze line. As soil freezes it changes dimensions or "heaves." Water is the only chemical compound that expands when it freezes. This is why icebergs float with about 90 percent of their bulk under water and 10 percent above. The part of the iceberg that is exposed represents the percentage that has expanded beyond its normal liquid dimension. Since frozen water has a larger volume than water in a liquid state, frozen water is less dense, so it floats. When water in soil freezes it also expands. If a foundation is built on top of the soil it may float across the soil as it shifts, so foundations are built with a footer. As long as the footer reaches soil that will not shift from freezing the foundation remains stable. Many homes in parts of the country where the soil freezes have basements.

Basement Foundations

Basements may be finished or unfinished. Sometimes they are fully underground, other times they are only partially buried, or buried only on certain sides of the home. Homes can also have a cellar which is an unfinished dirt basement. These buildings will generally have a raised foundation with a dirt hole.

Basements are more common in some parts of the country than others. Where soils freeze in winter, basements are more common because they are also the foundation. The foundation must reach below the level where the soil will freeze, otherwise the expansion and contraction that occurs will cause major shifting and structural damage. If the foundation has to extend below the freeze/thaw level, it is often not much more expensive to turn the foundation into a basement area.

The basement serves as a deep footer that extends the foundation below the freeze line. Community codes based on the depth of the freeze line determines the depth of the footer. If a foundation is built that does not extend deep enough to reach below the point where the soil freezes the building will shift. As the cycle of freezing and thawing repeats, the stress on the building results in cracking and the foundation may become too unstable to support the structure.

Of course basements have their own problems. Since they are below ground level, it is important that they have extremely good drainage or else they can be subject to another water-related condition called hydrostatic pressure. A basement foundation without good drainage has a tremendous amount of pressure on it when the surrounding soils fill with water. Since water weighs eight pounds per gallon there can be enough hydrostatic pressure on a poorly drained basement foundation to cause the walls to crack and heave inward. If the basement isn't watertight, it takes on water and floods. If the basement is watertight, but the water in the soil surrounding the basement can't escape, the basement may attempt to float, exerting a tremendous amount of upward pressure. This can result in the basement lifting the structure above it, resulting in the collapse of the building.

Probably one of the biggest problems in existing basements is dampness. It is not uncommon for improper grading or drainage to result in water entering through floor or wall penetrations.

Homes with basements are also more likely to have problems with radon gas entering the building. Since basements expose a much greater soil surface area to the interior of a structure than any other type of foundation, the concentration of radon gas also tends to be greater.

It is unlikely that climate changes resulting in drier soils and desert-like conditions will correct basement moisture problems. It may be that the amount of moisture entering your basement will decrease at certain times of the year, but it is unlikely that any changes would eliminate the risk of water entry year-round — especially when we consider that the changes resulting from global warming are likely to result in greater fluctuations in extreme weather. Even deserts still have flash floods.

If your basement is dry, you may be lucky and already have the necessary controls installed to keep it dry without further assistance in spite of global changes, or maybe only minor modifications are needed.

Typically installed drainage may not be enough. Ideally, underground basement walls would have a water-resistant coating and a free-flowing drainage path on their exterior side to allow any water getting next to the basement wall to freely drain downward and away from the building. The free-flowing drainage path is important so that sump pumps won't be necessary. Gravity-fed drainage continues to function when the power fails.

The use of sealant coatings on the interior side of a basement foundation is not a good idea for multiple reasons. First, it is unlikely to really stop water from entering. Secondly, if it does prevent water from entering enough hydrostatic pressure might build up to cause the basement foundation walls to heave or crack creating new pathways for the entry of moisture. The sealant may also lead to a condition called spalling, a deterioration of the masonry.

The different foundations described by Joe Lstiburek in his *Builder's Guides* and *Moisture Control Handbook* are all well drained whether they are basement, slab-on-grade or raised (Lstiburek). They should perform well regardless of shifts in climate zone provided the soil is stable.

Drainage

Drainage should always be installed "to daylight." This means that water around the foundation has an escape path, using gravity to flow away

Efflorescence and Spalling

Efflorescence is generally a white- or light-colored powdery salt deposit that forms on damp masonry surfaces. It is sometimes confused with mold growth, but mold requires an organic nutrient like cellulose. Efflorescence is especially common after flooding has saturated masonry materials or in situations with inadequate drainage. As moisture flows through brick, concrete block, stone and other masonry materials it carries dissolved salts along. When the water reaches the surface of the material it evaporates, depositing the salt on the surface of the material. As long as the moisture can escape and doesn't build up, the salt deposits are harmless, although unsightly. Placing a nutritive material such as gypsum wallboard against masonry materials exhibiting efflorescence will generally result in mold growth on the gypsum paper.

Some people have tried to halt the flow of moisture and salts by sealing the surface of the masonry. This reduces the flow of moisture and the salts no longer reach the surface where they can be seen. At first it may seem like a reasonable solution. The problem is the moisture flow still occurs, although at a reduced rate, so the salts continue to build up just under the layer of masonry instead of forming on the surface of the material. This sets up an osmotic gradient that can result in hydrostatic pressure causing the masonry to lose its structural integrity and slough away in a process called spalling. Most people have observed this in sidewalks or other cement with a thin layer of material that has come off in a sheet. Once the masonry has spalled, the flow of moisture and salts resumes and the efflorescence once again builds up on the surface. Repeated applications of sealant will repeatedly spall until the masonry's structural ☛

from the building to the surface. Ideally, foundations are constructed to allow natural drainage to daylight. In order to drain to daylight the lower footing of the foundation would need to have a drain installed that leads away from it at a downward minimum slope of one percent with the end of the drain opening to daylight so that it can drain using gravity. This of course requires the bottom of the foundation to sit higher than the area it is being drained to.

In some areas, it is not possible to drain to daylight in which case sump pumps are used to pump the water away from the foundation. Foundation pumps are also often used as a short cut to proper foundation drainage.

integrity has been damaged. Many historic buildings, foundations and basements have been significantly damaged by the application of sealants. A better method for dealing with efflorescence on masonry is to coat the offending surface with a parge coat of plaster. This is a plaster material that is slightly softer and more porous than the masonry. As the moisture flows through the masonry, it continues through the parge coat and evaporates from the surface, but the salts remain behind in the parge coat. Eventually, when the salts become concentrated enough, the parge coat will slough away from the masonry and require cleaning and recoating with another layer of parge plaster. Since it is the parge that sloughs off instead of the masonry spalling away, there is no loss of structural integrity or damage to the masonry. Parge coats can provide very attractive finishes and are often dyed with mineral pigments to add color to the surface.

RESTORATION CONSULTANTS, INC.

The back of this closet is a concrete block retaining wall. Moisture migrating through the block is leaving fluffy white salt deposits as the water evaporates.

This is fine until the power or the pump fails. If the condition isn't corrected quickly enough, the foundation may flood with the rising water or heave if the water freezes.

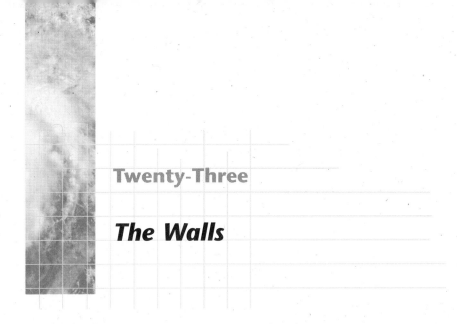

Twenty-Three

The Walls

In properly functioning buildings, the walls should act to keep water out while allowing water vapor to escape to prevent trapped vapor from resulting in damage and mold growth. As the climate changes the way a wall is constructed in different parts of the country will need to change in order to prevent damage. This chapter discusses how walls should function and how to recognize conditions that will lead to problems.

Some materials that may cause problems if incorrectly used in a building include vapor-retarding membranes and vapor barriers in the wrong place. Vinyl wallpaper can act as an unintended vapor barrier, as can various types of paints and sealants. When these materials are used incorrectly they can result in major damage to buildings. As climate changes occur materials that were correctly used originally may cease to function properly, resulting in damage to the walls and other building components.

This chapter also discusses ways to retrofit buildings to reduce or prevent damage that results from climate change. These retrofits may be as simple as stripping and replacing vinyl wallpaper with a breathable finish or more complicated, like increasing structural strength by adding framing straps or bolting the sill plate to the foundation.

The Ideal Wall

As long as the climate remained stable, it was possible to construct inexpensive energy efficient walls that were able to perform well in their specific climate zones. With climates shifting and becoming more unpredictable it is becoming more important for buildings to be able to deal with a wide variety of conditions. The advantages of heavy masonry walls have been discussed in earlier chapters; however, their construction is often expensive and not enough builders are experienced in these techniques. Another form of heavy-duty wall that has demonstrated its durability under a wide variety of climate conditions is straw-clay. This

The EcoNest is a modern adaptation of an ancient technique using timber framing and straw-clay infill to create an energy efficient vapor-permeable wall assembly.

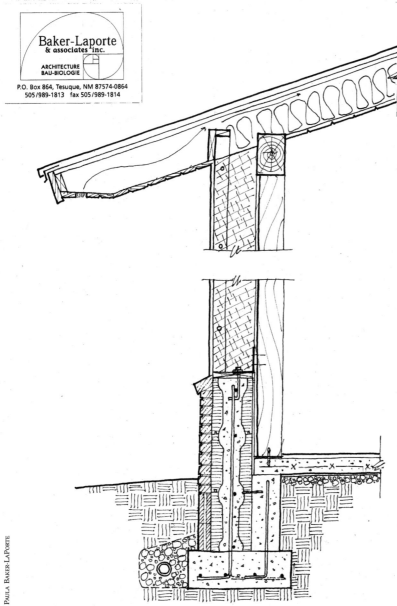

Baker-Laporte
& associates inc.

ARCHITECTURE
BAU-BIOLOGIE

P.O. Box 864, Tesuque, NM 87574-0864
505/989-1813   fax 505/989-1814

PAULA BAKER-LAPORTE

The EcoNest vapor-permeable wall is further protected from excess moisture accumulation by good drainage and roof overhangs.

form of construction has been reintroduced into North America and is advocated by my co-author Paula Baker LaPorte and her husband Robert LaPorte. In *Prescriptions for a Healthy House* we explained that straw-clay construction "uses a lightweight mixture of straw and clay as an 'outsulating' wall around a timber-frame structure. Straw-clay can also be used as an infill material between deep structural members. … Straw is mixed with a clay slurry so that each strand is coated. The wet material is then compacted into a 12" wide formwork. The formwork is removed the same day. The result is a precise wall that has enough texture to accept mud plaster without any further wall preparation or lathing" (Baker-LaPorte). Paula and Robert have a new book that further explains the advantages of straw-clay and how to build with it, titled *EcoNest: Creating Sustainable Sanctuaries of Clay Straw, and Timber*. These straw-clay structures are built to last centuries. The construction method has demonstrated its durability in various forms throughout many parts of the world. Straw-clay construction is labor intensive and is obviously not suited for the conventional construction industry. So, although I personally like and want to own a straw-clay home some day, I realize it will likely remain a niche market.

While searching for the ideal wall that could withstand climate change, I understood it needed to be able to be constructed with materials readily available from any lumber yard right now. The biggest issue for wall assemblies is moisture flow so that water vapor will always be able to escape and not accumulate. Smart vapor-retarding membranes are under development, but may be many years before they are readily available. My search led me to the US Department of Housing and Urban Development's National Institute of Standards and Technology. In January 1995, their Building and Fire Research Laboratory published a paper titled *Manufactured Housing Walls That Provide Satisfactory Moisture Performance in all Climates*. The study was prepared because manufactured homes were failing in certain parts of the country. Manufacturers of these prefabricated homes needed one wall assembly that would work in diverse climates such as Madison, Wisconsin; Miami, Florida; and Little Rock, Arkansas.

The wall is described as follows:

> The interior and exterior claddings of this wall consist of 12.7 mm (0.5 in.) exterior-grade plywood, sandwiching 89 mm (3.5 in.) glass-fiber insulation. The interior of this wall is finished with 7.9 mm (0.31 in.) gypsum board. Latex paint is applied to the interior and exterior surfaces. We call this wall a variable-permeance-claddings wall. The term "variable permeance" comes about from the moisture behavior of plywood. ... When plywood is exposed to ambient relative humidities below 50%, it performs as a vapor retarder. On the other hand, when plywood absorbs moisture and approaches saturation, it becomes very permeable.

The properties of exterior-grade plywood are exactly what were needed to "breathe" in both directions in exactly the right way. The study went on to explain the performance for the system in Madison, Wisconsin:

> The peak surface relative humidity is seen to occur at the inside surface of the exterior plywood layer during the middle of the winter and is seen to be below saturation (97%). This indicates that free liquid water is unlikely to be present in the pore structure of the construction materials. However, the surface relative humidity does at times exceed the critical 80% level, but concurrent temperatures are too low for mold and mildew growth. This construction is, therefore, likely to have satisfactory moisture performance during the cold winter climate, especially since this evaluation was conducted with

The plywood on both sides of a variable permeability wall has low permeability when the wall cavity is dry, but becomes more permeable when the wall cavity becomes wet.

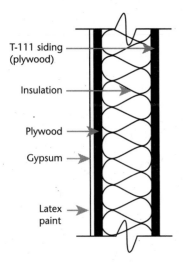

T-111 siding (plywood)

Insulation

Plywood

Gypsum

Latex paint

relatively high indoor humidity conditions. ... During the winter, the interior plywood layer functions as an interior vapor retarder and significantly reduces the ingress of moisture into the construction from the indoor environment.

They then repeated the modeling performance study of the wall for summer and determined that:

> During the early summer, moisture begins to accumulate in the interior plywood, increasing its permeance beyond that of the exterior plywood. As a result, the interior plywood is able to transfer moisture out of the wall cavity to the building interior faster than the exterior plywood is able to transfer moisture from the outdoor environment into the cavity. The relative humidity therefore remains below the critical level inside the wall. ... As the moisture content of the exterior plywood rises during the winter, its permeance increases, thereby permitting accumulated moisture to be transferred through the plywood to the outdoor environment.

They then evaluated the same variable-permeance-claddings wall for Miami, Florida concluding:

> All the surface relative humidities remained below the critical 80% RH level throughout the year, and we therefore would not expect any mold and mildew growth in this wall. During the early summer, moisture begins to accumulate in the interior plywood, increasing its permeance beyond that of the exterior plywood. As a result, the interior plywood is able to transfer moisture out of the wall cavity to the building interior faster than

the exterior plywood is able to transfer moisture from the outdoor environment into the cavity. The relative humidity therefore remains below the critical level inside the wall (Burch).

This demonstrated the wall assembly was practical for cold climates as well as hot-humid climates. Further studies confirmed it would also work in mixed-climates. The information in that paper can easily be adapted for new construction or post-disaster reconstruction for any part of the country. It is exactly what we need for buildings that will be able to withstand the shifts from climate change.

This is about as close to an ideal wall as we can come with current technology. One very important thing to always remember is that material specifications vary by manufacturer. Just because a wall system performs using one brand of exterior plywood doesn't necessarily mean all brands will work equally well. The paper was written in 1995 without any realization of its relevance to climate change. Two substitutions that are likely to improve the system are using DensArmor Plus instead of the interior paper-faced gypsum wallboard and T1-11 siding for the exterior plywood on the outside of the building. This should work since the permeability for T1-11 siding according to Roseburg Forest Products is the same as exterior-grade plywood. DensArmor Plus is reported by Georgia Pacific on their product hot line to have a permeability of 23 for their half-inch panels and 17 for their five-eighth-inch panels. This should work as a replacement for papered gypsum wallboard since the permeability of DensArmor Plus is higher than the permeability of the exterior-grade plywood that is installed directly underneath. Computer simulations of this and other potentially improved wall assemblies are being run and the results will be posted on www.extremeweatherhitshome.com when they are complete.

Most modern walls are actually constructed with a double exterior layer with a deliberate space between the layers for drainage. The outermost layer is a material that is durable when exposed to the outdoors. It provides the bulk of the protection against the direct elements. This layer is rarely watertight although the exterior of the building keeps out the bulk of water. The inner wall layer is commonly referred to as the "drain plane" since its primary purpose is to drain the water from the wall, preventing it from entering the wall cavity and insulation. The inner wall layer is frequently an impregnated felt material. It is supposed to be installed by overlapping the sheets of construction felt so that water drains downward and is directed towards the outside. The bottom of the wall will usually have a gap at the bottom so that if water does get

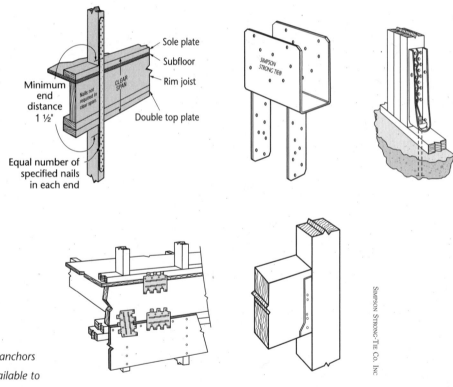

A variety of tie clips, anchors and fasteners are available to help stabilize the structure.

between the two layers of outer wall it has a drainage path so that it doesn't remain inside the wall. The opening at the bottom of the wall frequently has an expanded metal screen called a weep screed which helps keep insects and vermin from getting into the wall assembly but allows water to escape. If the construction felt wall layer is not properly installed, water may get into the inner wall cavity space where the insulation is installed. Any place where there are penetrations through the wall such as nail holes, wall outlets and plumbing pipes, there are increased risks of water being able to penetrate into the insulated part of the wall. These penetrations require installing additional layers of water-resistant, vapor-permeable material to direct water that gets behind the exterior cladding material back to the outside of the building. New peel and stick waterproof membranes have been developed. They are made of asphalt-based rubber bitumen that is self adhering, and can be very effective for sealing around doors, windows, penetrations and seams where materials join, but since they are vapor-impermeable they must not cover a significant portion of the breathable material to ensure they do not trap water vapor resulting in condensation in wall cavities. Roof overhangs can also help shield the walls, doors and windows from falling rain and snow and reduce the likelihood of water entry.

Increasing Structural Strength

A very important component of the ideal wall is that it must be fastened securely to its foundation. Older buildings usually aren't fastened to the foundation. Code now requires the walls in newer buildings be securely bolted to the foundation, but construction practices sometimes omit these fasteners, or they are installed in ways that are not as strong as they could be. Another concern is that not all fastening systems function equally well. Howard Cook of Bay Area Retrofit is a specialist in seismic retrofits for residential and commercial buildings. Because of earthquakes the San Francisco Bay area has served as a living laboratory for studying the performance of foundation bolts. A number of surprising facts have ☛

been discovered that are important not only in earthquake country, but should also apply to high winds and flooding.

Cook states:

> The Uniform Building Code (UBC) which is designed for new construction and is not intended for retrofit, specifies that only 5/8 inch bolts with plate washers may be used. They should be 6 ft. o.c. (on center) on single and two story homes. ... The most significant increase in strength in this connection was achieved by installing large square plate washers on the bolts instead of round cut washers. [Round washers were acting like a wedge and causing the wooden sill plate to fracture.] ... This one simple change resulted in a 60% increase in strength.

The sill anchor strength can be improved even more, he continues:

> Harlen Metal Products also came up with a type of washer called a Mudsill Plate that is designed to increase the strength of the wood-to-bolt connection. This hardware is so effective that the earthquake resistance of a bolt can be more than doubled by installing one of these washers on the top and one on the bottom of the mudsill. The UBC recognizes a 1/2 inch bolt with a standard washer as being able to resist 840 pounds of shear. ICC report #1148 recognizes that installing one of these washers on top of the mudsill increases that resistance to 1340 pounds, a 59% increase in strength, while installing these washers on both the top and bottom of the mudsill increases the bolt strength to 2040 pounds, a 143% increase in strength. That's pretty good for a fifty-cent piece of hardware (Cook).

After learning this I went out into my garage and checked the anchor bolts that were present. The washers were round. I'm not ready to punch holes in my home's walls to replace the round washers with the special rectangular ones, but I am planning on replacing those washers that are exposed in our unfinished garage. For under $10 I will be able to improve the chances my attached garage will remain intact and not cause the house roof to collapse in extreme weather. If I ever decide to do a major remodel on the house, I will seriously consider changing out the rest of the round washers.

The holding force of wall anchor bolts varies with the materials used and how they are installed. The use of a round washer has provided an experimentally measured holding force of 840 pounds.

This square washer was installed misaligned. When extreme force is applied to the building the sharp corner can dig into the wood sill plate, causing it to fracture.

Properly aligning the square anchor to the sill plate increases the holding force to 1,340 pounds. The holding force can be increased to 2,040 pounds by sandwiching the sill plate between two square anchor plates.

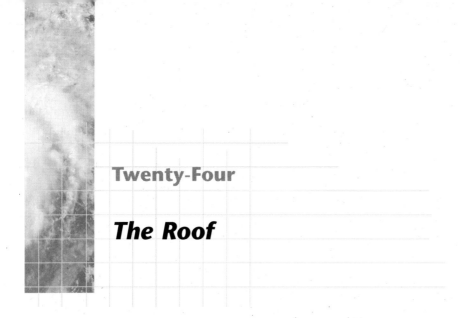

Twenty-Four

The Roof

It is very important that roofs function properly since they are typically the surface that takes the greatest beating. The roof protects the rest of the house from sun, rain, snow, sleet and hail. It is the surface that is most aerodynamic and likely to be lifted from the home by strong winds. If the structural supports of the roof are blown away, the rest of the house is likely to fold up and collapse like a house of cards. To find the ideal roof I began as I had before by looking at what has worked in different climate zones. Water needs to be allowed to shed, so the roofing shingles are overlapped allowing water to flow down and off the top of the roof. An underlayment of roofing felt is also overlapped so that if water penetrates the shingles, it is able to flow downward over the felt and off the roof without being able to enter into the building. Edges, seams and points where the roof forms valleys are the most likely problem places. An intricate roof is more likely to have a problem because it contains more trouble spots that require a perfect installation.

The Ideal Roof

The ideal roof would be resistant to sun, wind, fire, rain, snow, ice and hail. It would be reflective for energy conservation, breathable to prevent water vapor being trapped in all climates and durable. It appears there may be some challenges to developing one ideal roof that will perform under any condition. It appears that a better strategy would be to install a roof that will be likely to perform well under most circumstances. When extreme conditions occur, keeping the roof intact and the interior dry is the first and most important goal. A durable roof that remains intact is the ideal, but if the exterior roofing materials fail, then there should be a second line of defense to prevent water getting into the interior environment. The use of exterior-grade plywood, with hurricane clip fasteners to space and secure the panels for roof sheathing, can provide

The plywood panels for this roof assembly have been secured to one another using H-clip fasteners. Note that the peel and stick membrane only covers the plywood seams. Depending on the roofing materials used on top, this can create a roof assembly that can breathe, allowing moisture to dry and not be trapped.

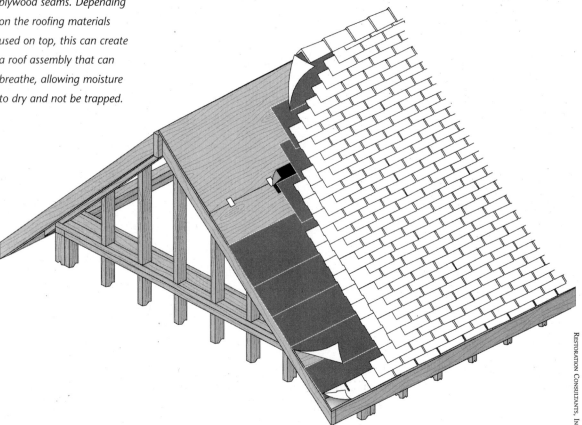

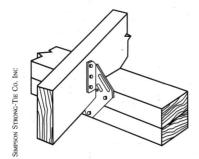

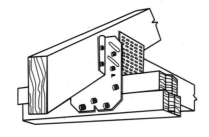

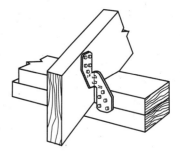

a good second line of defense and a very strong assembly. The seams for the joints between the plywood need to be sealed with the peel and stick membranes previously described.

A variety of ties are available for securing the roof to the walls.

The framing for the roof needs to be securely strapped to the walls to prevent the entire roof from being lifted off the building in one piece. Clemson University conducted post-hurricane field evaluations and was able to determine that "... once a few pieces of roof sheathing are gone, insurance claims on the order of 80 percent of the total value of the structure are typical" (Clemson), and that most of the damage is due to the water entry that occurs. This demonstrates the importance of secure sheathing, If your roof ends up sacrificing some shingles but the interior stays dry the repair costs will be minor in comparison.

The H-clip adds extra strength to the roof assembly and helps maintain the proper spacing between
plywood panels for expansion and contraction.

In order to minimize moisture condensation the attic should be eliminated or conditioned along with the rest of the building. Ideally humidity levels will be kept between 30 to 40 percent inside when extreme conditions are present outside. Even if the humidity goes above those levels for a couple of days the building should be able to recover as long as liquid water is kept out. The general concept would then

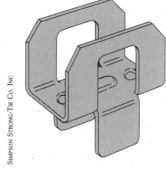

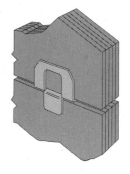

Secure Roofs

If you have a gable roof, it makes sense to add bracing to the attic floor and increase the nailing pattern for any wood panel attached to the gable end. The PATH Builders Association has made recommendations for the nail size, quantity and the nailing patterns that should be used to increase the strength and durability of construction. Their information is available from their website at: pathnet.org. They also are preparing best practice documents for recovering from floods and other disasters.

be to insulate the top side of the roof using rigid insulation to keep it thermally isolated from the warm interior. This helps ensure the dew point is not reached in materials sensitive to moisture. The rigid insulation would have a layer of plywood fastened on top and the finished roofing materials would be attached to the plywood. The R-value for the rigid insulation on top of the roof should be based on the cold temperature extreme that is anticipated. The details for such a roof installation go well beyond what can be described in this book. Joe Lstiburek's website at: buildingscience.com/resources/roofs/roofs_unvented, provides more details regarding this insulated roof. The colder the anticipated climate, the thicker the rigid insulation that needs to be installed.

When extreme temperatures are encountered the attic humidity can be monitored and adjustments made to reduce levels to the point where potential condensation issues can be avoided. Reducing humidity can be done by mechanical dehumidification. In an emergency, such as when the power is out, lifestyle changes can reduce indoor moisture levels. These include limiting the number and duration of showers, increasing the ventilation rate in the bathroom until the humidity is dissipated, keeping pots of boiling water covered and avoiding wet-mopping floors.

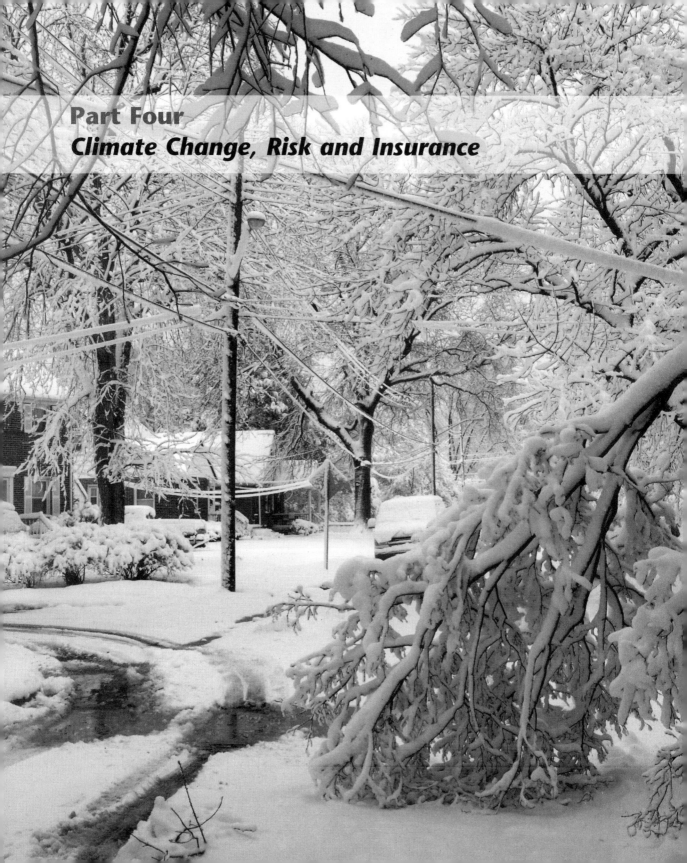

Part Four
Climate Change, Risk and Insurance

Twenty-Five

Insurance, Financial Impacts and Assistance

Our homes are generally one of the most expensive investments we will ever make. Extreme weather conditions as a result of climate change are increasing the risks of our investments being destroyed. Most of this book has been about preventing or limiting damage to our homes by understanding the potential effects of climate change and the extra stresses that are developing as a result.

Unfortunately some conditions will always exceed our ability to prepare our buildings to survive them. For those catastrophic cases our primary responsibility is to be sure we can protect our families. Insurance can help us recover financially from disasters, but it is important to remember that not every situation is covered. There are generally exclusions and deductibles that need to be understood.

> **Did You Know?**
>
> Over the course of a thirty year mortgage the risk of having a home flooded is estimated to be 26 percent. The risk of fire during the same period is only four percent.
>
> — Federal Emergency Management Agency

Understanding the Limits of Home Insurance

Insurance is one of the ways people minimize their risk of financial loss. We pay money to a company that pools our money with other people's money in order to redistribute that money when an insured loss occurs.

"Poor communities can be especially vulnerable, in particular those concentrated in high-risk areas. They tend to have more limited adaptive capacities, and are more dependent on climate-sensitive resources such as local water and food supplies."

(IPCC 2007 page 7
Summary for Policymakers)

Insurance companies don't gamble. They work very hard to understand both the risks and how much money is needed to cover those risks and still make a profit. For the most part, insurance companies don't cover the really big risks. Earthquake or flood insurance is usually purchased through a government program. The government covers the risk and the insurance carrier merely acts as the go-between to handle paperwork and collect money. The insurance carrier may act as a front and offer the government program to their policy holders, but if a claim is filed for these types of losses, the claim is with the government.

"All Peril" Coverage?

I have been a homeowner for 25 years. During this period our home has always been insured with a type of policy called "all peril." However, "all peril" does not mean it covers every possible type of damage. Typically, there are exclusions such as flood and earthquake. In spite of the work that I perform as an environmental consultant specializing in mold and water damage, until I began the research for this book, I have never had our home insured against flood damage. Our home wasn't in a flood zone, so it seemed unnecessary. My understanding of the risks was naive. According to the Federal Emergency Management Agency almost 25 percent of all flood insurance claims come from areas with minimal flood risk. Today our home has all of the standard types of insurance coverage that are readily available. I already had "all peril" insurance, but now I have also purchased flood and earthquake insurance. Our home is now truly insured from "all perils" like fire, water damage, flood, windstorms, lightning, hail and earthquakes.

Still, I wanted to find out just how protected my investment is and how my coverage relates to the additional risks presented by climate change. As I began to review the language in my home insurance policies I learned some general information that is important. (Please be aware that policy language can vary, and what is true for my policy may not apply to you.)

- The insurance company can refuse to renew my policy for any reason when it expires.

- My insurance policy can be canceled with 30 days notice from the carrier if there is a substantial change increasing the hazard risk.

- I must take reasonable steps to preserve my property from loss.

- Anything I do that increases a risk or hazard is not insured.

- My policy does not cover situations where there are two or more causes of loss to the property and the predominant cause of loss is excluded in the policy. (Whoa, that's a tough one and we'll need to come back to this).

- My policy excludes weather conditions that contribute with a cause of loss that is excluded where a loss occurs. (This isn't much better than the last: we will discuss this further.)

- If I have a loss I must give the insurance carrier immediate written notice, even if I don't file a claim.

- I must protect my property from further damage and make repairs necessary to protect it.

- I must show the insurance company the damage.

The way I read my policy regarding two or more causes of loss is best explained by an example. If my home were located in the Sacramento River Delta area (it's not) and high winds tore the roof off my house *and* damaged the levees protecting much of Sacramento so that my home flooded, the wind damage would not be covered by my "all peril" homeowners policy if 51 percent of the damage was

"Where extreme weather events become more intense and/or more frequent, the economic and social costs of those events will increase, and these increases will be substantial in the areas most directly affected."

(IPCC 2007 page 7 Summary for Policymakers)

due to the flood from the levee break. The flood damage would only be covered if I had the supplemental flood insurance and the program didn't run out of money. This is the very situation that many of the victims of Katrina in New Orleans face. Those who didn't have flood insurance have found themselves totally uninsured for both the flood and wind, at least until the courts interpret this differently. Those with flood insurance found that their payments were halted in September 2005 when the fund ran out of money. Congress later authorized payments to be resumed at the end of November 2005 when additional authority to borrow money was granted to the fund (FEMA).

My policy also excludes weather conditions that cause damage when another excluded condition occurs. In order to understand this better it will be necessary to look at what my "all perils" policy excludes (your policy language may differ).

- My policy won't pay for any kind of flooding that flows across the ground outside the building even if the water is driven by wind.
- There is no coverage for any kind of sewage backups, sump pump failures, seepage, leakage or subsurface water entering the building.
- Earth movement of any kind is excluded, as are all soil conditions including those that cause settling, cracking, shrinkage or expansion.
- The collapse of my home is only covered if the cause of the collapse is covered.
- All contaminants and pollution are excluded.
- Mold is excluded unless it develops as a result of a covered loss in which case the total payment is capped at $5,000.
- Frozen plumbing is excluded if I am away from my home, unless I keep my home heated or I have taken steps to drain my plumbing system and appliances while I am away.
- All foundation damage from freezing, thawing, hydrostatic pressure, adfreezing and wind conditions is excluded.

- My furnishings and personal property inside the house are not covered if they are damaged by rain, snow or sleet, unless a covered loss first damages the roof or walls and allows the water into the building.

Contaminant Exclusions

Another important policy considerations to look for is whether the policy has pollution exclusion. This basically states the carrier has no responsibility for paying for contaminants released into an indoor environment. These may include mold spores, asbestos, lead-based paint, fuel spills and a wide variety of different conditions that can be very expensive to fix. One very expensive contamination that insurance companies frequently won't pay for is sewage flowing from a municipal septic main. The insurance company denies coverage by claiming the sewage came from the sewer lines and not from a blockage on your property itself. If it was from a clog in your lines on your property, the policy may or may not pay for the decontamination. Of course with sewage coming from the whole neighborhood there is a greater likelihood of dangerous organisms making your family sick.

"Magnitudes of impact can now be estimated more systematically for a range of possible increases in global average temperature."

(IPCC 2007 page 12 Summary for Policymakers)

The flow of sewage as it backflows through a sewer system can often be prevented by a back-flow prevention valve. Some communities will take responsibility for sewage that flows from the municipal sewage system into a building; however, many communities refuse to take responsibility for sewage backflows if a back-flow prevention valve isn't installed and properly maintained. Some cities and municipalities will deny they have any responsibility regardless of the presence of back-flow prevention.

Another exclusion from most policies is for soil removal. If sewage inundates a crawlspace under a building, removing soil to correct the problem is typically excluded from the policy. The organic material found in sewage along with the bacterial contamination will generally result in an overpowering odor problem that can be difficult to eliminate.

The flood insurance I have purchased supplements my "all perils" policy, but still has exclusions for any form of earth movement, pollution, chemical contamination and "avoidable mold."

Earth Movement Exclusions

My earthquake insurance only covers damage caused by "seismic events" (earthquakes) and has a ten percent deductible. All other forms of earth movement are excluded. This means I can't get any form of readily available insurance for any form of soil movement involving expansive clay soils, melting permafrost (not a problem in California — yet), adfreezing, heat waves, desertification, drought or trapped moisture.

There may be some coverage for some of the damage that could be caused by these conditions. For example, expansive soil damage to the building is not covered. However, if expansive soils result in a sudden and accidental bursting of pipes, the water damage would likely be covered. The same would be true for any other condition causing a shifting that caused pipes to break suddenly releasing water, such as melting permafrost, adfreezing or broken pipes from freeze/thaw movement. The water damage is probably covered but the plumbing repair and the damage from the shifting is not. But — wait a minute — my policy also excludes situations where there are two or more causes of loss to the property and the predominant cause is excluded.

Flood Exclusions

If a flood results in water rushing into my home, it's covered under the flood policy, but my fences, retaining walls, doghouse and sheds aren't covered. If that flood water undermines the soil and the hillside slips, the damage to my home from the earth movement is not covered. If the soil needs to be stabilized to prevent the house from being damaged by slippage, I'm on my own. When it comes to extreme weather events, the different scenarios that can occur and the confusing nature of what is and isn't covered mean a good possibility of the loss being partially or wholly excluded. It is somewhat mind-boggling trying to sort it all out.

Rising sea levels would not be covered by the "all perils" policy but may be covered by the flood policy. It is unlikely that flood coverage would be continued with entire communities going under. The funds simply wouldn't be present and the programs would collapse or the conditions would be excluded. Since sea level rise occurs slowly there would be plenty of time for the flood programs to be changed or dropped, or the carriers not to renew.

The United States insurance industry has already begun to cancel or refuse to renew policies for insureds who have already suffered water damage. Consumers' insurance history is now tracked by over 600 insurance companies that report to a common data base called the Comprehensive Liability Underwriters Exchange (CLUE). When you report a loss, your information and the property information is entered into this data base and tracked. Based on your insurance loss history you may find it difficult, or very expensive, to get continuing coverage for your damaged property or any new properties you may own in the future. In addition, when you go to sell your previously damaged property, the new owner may not be able to get it affordably insured resulting in the sale falling through. You can get a copy of your CLUE report for your own home at www.choicetrust.com for $12.95.

According to Tim Flannery in *The Weather Makers*:

> Both insurance industry and climate trends suggest that householders ... whose weather-related deductible may now be in the hundreds of dollars, may soon be facing deductibles in the thousands or tens of thousands of dollars. The rising bills result largely from the laws of physics. Consider, for example, the impact of wind speed. An increase in wind speed during a storm from 40-50 knots to 50-60 knots increases building damage

by 650%. Similar escalations apply to extreme events as diverse as hurricanes, wildfires, floods, and heat waves. With all of these events projected to increase, the rapid escalation of insurance bills is unavoidable (Flannery).

Different insurance carriers have adopted different positions regarding what buildings they will cover. For example, State Farm announced at the end of 2006 it would not renew policies for any home within 2,500 feet of coastal waters or bays. They will not offer new policies to anyone within a mile of the coast. Allstate on the other hand is eliminating the wind coverage for about 65,000 homeowners along the coast. (Insurance Newsnet) In May 2007 Allstate announced that it would not write new policies for home owners in the state of California, saying "it fears the threat of costly natural disasters" (Chan).

What Will the Government Do for You?

Since insurance coverage doesn't cover many of the possible consequences of climate change related damage, we should look at what government programs may provide.

- Federal disaster relief programs are designed to help you get partly back on your feet but not to replace everything you lose.
- The Department of Homeland Security's Federal Emergency Management Agency (FEMA) is tasked with responding to, planning for and mitigating disasters.
- After the President signs a major disaster declaration, FEMA cooperates with other agencies, such as the Small Business Administration (SBA), in providing disaster relief.
- The primary form of disaster relief is low-interest loans to eligible individuals, homeowners and businesses made available through the SBA to repair or replace damaged property and personal belongings not covered by insurance.

- The maximum SBA personal property loan is $40,000, and the maximum SBA real property loan for primary home repair is $200,000.
- FEMA disaster grants for emergency home repairs and temporary rental assistance are only available to individuals and households who do not qualify for loans.
- The average FEMA grant is less than $15,000 (the maximum is $26,200) — not enough to rebuild a home in the San Francisco Bay Area, or any other part of California.
- The Farm Service Agency (FSA) offers loans to assist agricultural businesses.

As problems from global warming continue to expand it is likely we will also see changes in the way that FEMA and other government disaster assistance programs disburse their funds. Eventually, if global warming and climate change aren't controlled, the amount of damage likely to occur will become so widespread that these assistance programs are likely to cease to exist or have drastic shortages.

"Many estimates of aggregate net economic costs of damages from climate change across the globe (i.e., the social cost of carbon (SCC), expressed in terms of future net benefits and costs that are discounted to the present) are now available. Peer-reviewed estimates of the SCC for 2005 have an average value of US$43 per tonne of carbon (tC) (i.e., US$12 per tonne of carbon dioxide) but the range around this mean is large. It is very likely that globally aggregated figures underestimate the damage costs because they cannot include many non-quantifiable impacts. Taken as a whole, the range of published evidence indicates that the net damage costs of climate change are likely to be significant and to increase over time."

(IPCC 2007 page 16
Summary for Policymakers)

Twenty-Six

Conclusions

I think the environment should be put in the category of our national security. Defense of our resources is just as important as defense abroad. Otherwise what is there to defend?
— Robert Redford

The October 12, 2006 edition of the *New Scientist* reported that if people were to immediately and completely stop burning all petrochemicals,

about 15 percent of the CO_2 from burning fossil fuels will remain in the atmosphere, leaving its concentration at about 300 parts per million compared with pre-industrial levels of 280ppm. "There will be CO_2 left in the atmosphere continuing to influence the climate, more than 1000 years after humans stop emitting it," says Susan Solomon, an atmospheric chemist with the US National Oceanic and Atmospheric Administration (NOAA) in Boulder, Colorado.

Even if CO_2 emissions stop tomorrow, though, global warming will continue for another century, boosting

"Adaptation will be necessary to address impacts resulting from the warming which is already unavoidable due to past emissions."

(IPCC 2007 page 17 Summary for Policymakers)

average temperatures by a further few tenths of a degree. Atmospheric scientists call this "committed warming," and it happens because the oceans take so long to warm up compared with the atmosphere. …We can't just stop and expect everything to be OK, because we're already committed to this warming (Holmes).

This means we need to begin to prepare for the inevitable changes now.

Over the centuries forward thinkers have predicted events that may have dire consequences for the inhabitants of this planet. Sometimes there is a rallying response and other times the individual is labeled insane. Eventually the facts sort themselves out so the truth becomes clear.

We have become a "just in time" society with cellular communication, instant messaging and next day delivery. When it comes to global warming from man-made carbon dioxide emissions we are not "just in time"; the crisis is already here.

There are those who claim the extreme weather events that are becoming very apparent are nothing more than a normal cycle. I personally don't believe this, but even if that is true, it doesn't change what we need to do. We are still in crisis, and reducing our carbon emissions would certainly help get even a natural crisis under control.

Even a massive response isn't going to change conditions immediately, so we need to prepare. With some innovation, some luck and a lot of hard work, we may be able to find our way to a period where the planet settles into a gentler cycle, but it is going to take a while. The year 2004 brought hurricanes Charley, Francis and Ivan. It was a bad year for extreme weather, but it was topped by 2005. Hurricane Katrina trumped all of the other storms in terms of damages, but it was only one of a record-setting 27 hurricanes affecting North America. *BusinessWeek.com* has estimated Katrina's costs alone could top $200 billion (Wyss). Things

> "A wide array of adaptation options is available, but more extensive adaptation than is currently occurring is required to reduce vulnerability to future climate change. There are barriers, limits and costs, but these are not fully understood."
>
> (IPCC 2007 page 17 Summary for Policymakers)

> "Although many early impacts of climate change can be effectively addressed through adaptation, the options for successful adaptation diminish and the associated costs increase with increasing climate change."
>
> (IPCC 2007 page 17 Summary for Policymakers)

started out slow for hurricanes in 2006 — but not for other extreme weather conditions. By year's end, 2006 proved to be the warmest year on record. Triple-digit temperatures broke records across North America. In August, thunderstorm activity resulted in grapefruit-sized hailstones raining down in North Dakota. September began with an unusual West Coast hurricane called John which hammered the coast of Baja California, weakening to a tropical storm that still caused heavy rains and some flooding by the time it reached the United States. Early wet ice storms in New York resulted in lifetime residents of Buffalo seeing more damage than they had ever observed.

Most authorities now agree that extreme weather is a fact. As I travel around North America talking with people there is widespread recognition amongst the general public that all is not right with our climate, along with a desire, at least sometimes, to identify and correct the situation. Political action is often slow. Private enterprise can respond much more quickly, but many responses by business people and politicians are likely to be too narrowly focused. In the 1970s we responded to the energy crisis by adding insulation and tightening up our houses. Some of the early attempts at solar heating for water and our homes were somewhat poorly planned or tested. The retrofits often created more damage than they corrected. The intent was good, but the application was faulty. Gradually system failures led to an understanding of what did and didn't work. It is now time to apply what we have learned to begin to respond to the threat of global warming. The extreme weather events of the last few years have come on rather suddenly. We always had occasional disasters, but now they are often back-to-back. Long-term trends and projections don't foresee specifics. The extreme fluctuations that are being experienced world-wide make predicting the future practically impossible, so flexibility remains very important.

Many of this book's suggestions are simple and easy to implement. Others may be more costly and require some planning. No changes to your home should be made frivolously or without a good understanding

"Adaptation alone is not expected to cope with all the projected effects of climate change, and especially not over the long run as most impacts increase in magnitude."
(IPCC 2007 page 17 Summary for Policymakers)

of the reason for the change and the potential ramifications. Some of the suggestions made in this book will not apply to every situation. I have made my best effort to be current and correct, but many of the variables we face go well beyond today's predictions. You should consult professionals to help identify your situation and the necessary corrections. It is important to always keep this in mind when you are making any remodeling decisions. I hope this book has provided the basic information so you will be able ask the necessary questions to help your projects succeed.

We are on a fast-track learning curve. Open communication can assist in monitoring the extreme weather events and climate changes that are occurring. One way of staying informed and up to date is the Internet. The website www.extremeweatherhitshome.com has been established to serve as an information hub and to provide additional updates and resources. By sharing our successes and learning from our failures we can help lessen our individual burdens. This web site provides links to resources discussed in this book as well as additional information updates for the future. The very nature of publishing a book guarantees that some of the information, for example regarding material use and availability, will be out of date by the time you read it. It is my hope that the Internet will help to facilitate the rapid expansion of our knowledge to help us through these troubling times. I want to hear and share your successes and your failures as we move forward into this uncertain future.

"Sustainable development can reduce vulnerability to climate change by enhancing adaptive capacity and increasing resilience. At present, however, few plans for promoting sustainability have explicitly included either adapting to climate change impacts, or promoting adaptive capacity. On the other hand, it is very likely that climate change can slow the pace of progress toward sustainable development either directly through increased exposure to adverse impact or indirectly through erosion of the capacity to adapt."

(IPCC 2007 page 18
Summary for Policymakers)

References

Introduction

Phil Camp. "Expanding Soils and Shrink-Swell Potential." *Understanding Soil Risks and Hazards: Using Soil Survey to Identify Areas with Risks and Hazards to Human Life and Property.* Gary B. Muckel, ed., United States Department of Agriculture, Natural Resources Conservation Service, National Soil Survey Center, 2004.

Chapter 1: Why Good Buildings Go Bad

ACGIH, *Bioaerosols: Assessment and Control.* American Conference of Governmental Industrial Hygienists, 1999.

Chapter 2: How Homes are Damaged by Climate Change

William E. Easterling III, Brian H. Hurd and Joel B. Smith. *Coping with Global Climate Change: The Role of Adaptation in the United States.* Pew Center on Global Climate Change, 2004.

James Hansen. "Warming Expert: Only decade left to act in time," MSNBC News Services, msnbc.msn.com/id/14834318/ (Cited April 21, 2007).

Charles Keller, Manvendra Dubey and Howard Hanson. *A cooling troposphere and global warming can co-exist.* Los Alamos National Laboratory Atmospheric and Climate Sciences Group. American Geophysical Union's fall meeting, December 16, 1999.

William B. Rose. *Water in Buildings: An Architect's Guide to Moisture and Mold.* John Wiley & Sons, 2005.

Chapter 3: Wind Storms

NASA, Tropical Rainfall Measuring Mission. trmm.gsfc.nasa.gov/publications_dir/south_atlantic_cyclone.html. Cited September 30, 2006.

NASA, Hurricane Archives. www.nasa.gov/mission_pages/hurricanes/archives/2006/trmm_2006rain.html. Cited September 30, 2006.

Tim Flannery. *The Weather Makers: How Man is Changing the Climate and What it Means for Life on Earth.* Atlantic Monthly Press, 2006.

Tore Jakobsen and Jeff Wimmer. "Coping With Spring Weather Claims." *Claims,* June 2001.

Clemson University. "What Homeowners Can Do To Make Their Homes Stronger Against High Winds." www.clemson.edu/special/hugo/index. Cited September 30, 2006.

Chapter 4: Tornados

NOAA Tornado Climatology. NOAA Satellite and Information Services, National Environmental Satellite, Data, and Information Services. www.ncdc.noaa.gov/oa/climate/severeweather/tornadoes. Cited September 26, 2006.

NOAA Storm Prediction Center. *Intense Supercell over Mexico.* www.spc.noaa.gov/coolimg/del_rio/index. Cited December 13, 2006.

Chapter 5: Hurricanes

Tim Flannery. *The Weather Makers.* Atlantic Monthly Press, 2006.

P.J. Webster, G.J. Holland, J.A. Curry and H.-R. Chang. "Changes in Tropical Cyclone Number, Duration, and Intensity in a Warming Environment." *Science* 16 September 2005.

Chapter 6: Lightning

Richard Kithil. *Annual USA Lightning Costs and Losses.* www.lightningsafety.com/nlsi_lls/nlsi_annual_usa_losses. Cited September 24, 2006.

Red Cross. *Talking About Disaster: Guide for Standard Messages.* National Disaster Education Coalition, 1999. www.redcross.org/services/disaster/keepsafe/wildfire.html#cause. Cited September 24, 2006.

Steven Winter. *The Rehab Guide: Site Work.* US Department of Housing and Urban Development, Office of Policy Development and Research Affordable Housing, Research and Technology Division, August 2000.

Chapter 8: Flooding

Institute of Inspection, Cleaning and Restoration Certification. *IICRC S500 Standard and Reference Guide for Professional Water Damage Restoration, 3rd ed.,* 2006.

M. Berry et al. "Suggested Guidelines for Remediation of Damage from Sewage Backflow into Buildings." *Journal of Environmental Health,* 57, 1994.

T. Straub et al. "Hazards from Pathogenic Microorganisms in Land-disposed Sewage Sludge." *Reviews of Environmental Contamination and Toxicology,* 1993.

Institute of Inspection, Cleaning and Restoration Certification. *IICRC S520 Standard and Reference Guide for Professional Mold Remediation,* 2003.

R.G. Feachem et al., *Appropriate Technology for Water Supply and Sanitation.* Energy, Water and Telecommunications Department of the World Bank, 1980.

US EPA. *Mold Remediation in Schools and Commercial Buildings.* United States Environmental Protection Agency, Office of Air and Radiation, Indoor Environments Division, 2001.

K. A. Reynolds. "Efficacy of sodium hypochlorite disinfectant on the viability and allergenic properties of household mold." *Journal of Allergy and Clinical Immunology,* Volume 113, Issue 2, February 2004.

Chapter 9: Rising Temperatures

Qiang Fu et al. "Faster Enhanced Mid-Latitude Tropospheric Warming in Satellite Measurements." *Science,* May 26, 2006.

C. Rosenzweig et al. *Mitigating New York City's Heat Island with Urban Forestry, Living Roofs, and Light Surfaces.* Presentation at 86th American Meteorological Society Annual Meeting, January 2006.

J.S. Kirkpatrick and M.D. Shulman. "A Statistical Evaluation of the New York City–Northern New Jersey Urban Heat Island Effect on Summer Daily Minimum Temperature." *National Weather Digest*, 12(1), 1987.

Chapter 10: Drought and Desertification

Tim Flannery. *The Weather Makers.* Atlantic Monthly Press, 2006.

Chapter 11: Heat Wave

Janet Larsen. *Setting the Record Straight: More than 52,000 Europeans Died from Heat in Summer 2003.* Earth Policy Institute, July 28, 2006, www.earth-policy.org/Updates/2006/Update56.htm. Cited September 19, 2006.

Gerald A. Meehl and Claudia Tebaldi. *More intense, more frequent, and longer lasting heat waves in the 21st century.* National Center for Atmospheric Research, August 2004

Compu Weather Weekly Highlights. *Weather Highlights: The Long Hot Summer.* www.compuweather.com/weather-newsletter.html. Cited September 20, 2006.

NASA. *2005 Warmest Year in Over a Century.* www.nasa.gov/vision/earth/environment/2005_warmest.html. Cited October 5, 2006.

Sonia Seneviratne. "Land-Atmosphere Coupling and Climate Change in Europe." *Nature*, September 14, 2006.

Chapter 12: Fires

A.L. Westerling and T.W. Swetnam. "Warming and Earlier Spring Increases Western US Forest Wildfire Activity." *Science*, August 18, 2006.

Institute for Business and Home Safety. "Protect Your Home Against Wildfire Damage." www.ibhs.org/publications/downloads/125.pdf. Cited September 16, 2006.

Chapter 13: Expansive Soils

FEMA. *Multi-Hazard Risk Identification and Assessment.* www.fema.gov/txt/fhm/mhira_n2.txt. Cited April 27, 2007.

J.J. Hamilton. "Foundations on Swelling or Shrinking Subsoils." *Canadian Building Digest,* March 1977.

United Facilities Criteria. *Foundations in Expansive Soils.*, UFC 3-220-07. January 2004.

W.W. Olive et al. *Swelling Clays Map Of The Conterminous United States.* US Geological Survey, 1989.

D.M. Robinson. *Maintenance Recommendations For Foundations On Expansive Clay Soil.* www.profengineering.com/fndcare.htm. Cited April 14, 2007.

D.E. Jones, Jr. and W.G. Holtz. "Expansive Soils: The Hidden Disaster." *Civil Engineering,* v. 43, no. 8, 1973.

Chapter 14: Melting Permafrost

Robert Roy Britt. "Surprising Side Effects of Global Warming." *LiveScience 22,* December 2004. www.livescience.com/forcesofnature/041222_permafrost.html. Cited September 27, 2006.

Neil Thomas. *Geocryology important tool in global change science.* www.udel.edu/PR/experts/geocryology.html. Cited September 30, 2006.

Molly Bentley. *Earth's permafrost starts to squelch.* BBC News, December 29, 2004. http://news.bbc.co.uk/2/hi/science/nature/4120755.stm. Cited May 1, 2007.

Sun Zhizhong, Ma Wei and Li Dongqing. "In situ test on cooling effectiveness of air convection embankment with crushed rock slope protection in permafrost regions." *Journal of Cold Regions Engineering,* vol. 19, no. 2, 2005.

US Global Change Research Program. *Adaptation Options for Impacts from Thawing Permafrost and Melting Sea Ice.* www.usgcrp.gov/usgcrp/nacc/education/alaska/ak-edu-3.htm. Cited September 27, 2006.

Chapter 15: Rising Sea Level

ACIA. *Impacts of a Warming Arctic.* Arctic Climate Impact Assessment, 2004. http://amap.no/acia. Cited September 8, 2006.

Tim Flannery. *The Weather Makers.* Atlantic Monthly Press, 2006.

NASA Earth Observatory. *Elevation of Southern Florida.* http://earthobservatory.nasa.gov/Newsroom/NewImages/ images.php3?img_id = 16663. Cited October 10, 2006.

US Environmental Protection Agency. *US Climate Action Report 2002.* www.epa.gov/globalwarming/publications/car/index.html. Cited September 8, 2006.

Al Gore. *An Inconvenient Truth.* Rodale Press, 2006.

Chapter 16: Trapped Moisture

Joseph Lstiburek and John Carmody. *Moisture Control Handbook: Principles and Practices for Residential and Small Commercial Buildings.* John Wiley & Sons, 1994.

Chapter 17: Freezing

Larry Jacobson and Kevin Janni. *Snow, ice raise concerns about excessive roof loads on farm buildings.* University of Minnesota Extension Service, December 24, 1996. www.extension.umn.edu/extensionnews/2005/snowload07.html. Cited February 28, 2007.

E. Penner and K.N. Burn. *Adfreezing and Frost Heaving of Foundations.* National Research Council of Canada, August 1970. http://irc.nrc-cnrc.gc.ca/pubs/cbd/cbd128-print_e.html. Cited September 7, 2006.

Chapter 19: Frozen Plumbing

William B. Rose. *Water in Buildings: An Architect's Guide to Moisture and Mold.* John Wiley & Sons, 2005.

Chapter 20: Earthquakes

Göran Ekström, Meredith Nettles and Victor C. Tsai. "Seasonality and Increasing Frequency of Greenland Glacial Earthquakes." *Science,* March 24, 2006.

Chapter 21: The Building Site

US Environmental Protection Agency. *A Citizen's Guide to Radon: The Guide to Protecting Yourself and Your Family From Radon.* www.epa.gov/radon/pubs/citguide.html. Cited May 28, 2007.

Chapter 22: The Foundation

Joseph Lstiburek and John Carmody. *Moisture Control Handbook.* John Wiley & Sons, 1994.

Joseph Lstiburek. *Builder's Guide: Cold Climates.* Energy Efficient Building Association and Shelter Source, 1997.

Joseph Lstiburek. *Builder's Guide: Mixed-Humid Climates.* Energy Efficient Building Association and Shelter Source, 1997.

Joseph Lstiburek. *Builder's Guide: Hot-Dry and Mixed-Dry Climates.* Energy Efficient Building Association and Shelter Source, 1997.

Joseph Lstiburek. *Builder's Guide: Hot-Humid Climates.* Energy Efficient Building Association and Shelter Source, 1997.

Chapter 23: The Walls

Paula Baker-LaPorte, Erica Elliott, MD and John Banta. *Prescriptions for a Healthy House: A Practical Guide for Architects, Builders and Homeowners.* New Society Publishers, 2001.

Paula Baker-Laporte and Robert Laporte, *EcoNest: Creating Sustainable Sanctuaries of Clay, Straw and Timber.* Gibbs Smith, 2005.

Douglas M. Burch, Christopher A. Saunders and Anton TenWolde. *Manufactured Housing Walls That Provide Satisfactory Moisture Performance in all Climates.* US Department of Housing and Urban Development, National Institute of Standards and Technology, 1995.

Howard Cook. *Bay Area Retrofit.* www.bayarearetrofit.com/RetrofitDesign/Bolting/bolting. Cited October 29, 2006.

Chapter 24: The Roof

Clemson University. *What Homeowners Can Do To Make Their Homes Stronger Against High Winds.* www.clemson.edu/special/hugo/index. Cited September 30, 2006.

Chapter 25: Financial Impacts

FEMA. *Insurance Payments Resume to Katrina Victims.*
www.fema.gov/news/newsrelease.fema?id = 20872.
Cited October 31, 2006.

Tim Flannery. *The Weather Makers.* Atlantic Monthly Press, 2006.

Insurance Newsnet. www.insurancenewsnet.com.
Cited September 18, 2006.

Gilbert Chan. "No New Policies in State." *The Sacramento Bee,*
May 11, 2007.

USGS. *Putting Down Roots in Earthquake Country: Your Handbook for
the San Francisco Bay Region.* http://pubs.usgs.gov/gip/2005/15.
Cited May 28, 2007.

Chapter 26: Conclusions

Bob Holmes. "Imagine Earth Without People." *New Scientist,* October
12, 2006.

David Wyss, "A Second Look at Katrina's Costs." *BusinessWeek Online,*
September 13, 2005. www.businessweek.com/bwdaily/dnflash/
sep2005/nf20050913_8975_db082.htm. Cited October 31, 2006.

Resources and Essential Reading

Essential Reading

General

Richard Heinberg. *The Party's Over: Oil, War, and the Fate of Industrial Societies.* New Society Publishers, 2005.

Guy Dauncey and Patrick Mazza. *Stormy Weather: 101 Solutions to Global Climate Change.* New Society Publishers, July 2001.

Al Gore. *An Inconvenient Truth.* Rodale Press, May 2006.

Godo Stoyke. *The Carbon Buster's Home Energy Handbook: Slowing Climate Change and Saving Money.* New Society Publishers, November 2006.

Flooding

Institute of Inspection, Cleaning and Restoration Certification. *IICRC S500 Standard and Reference Guide for Professional Water Damage Restoration, 3rd ed.* IICRC, 2006.

Fire

National Interagency Fire Center. *Protecting Your Home from Wildland Fire.* www.nifc.gov/preved/protecthome.html. Accessed August 18, 2006.

Firewise Communities. *Firewise Construction and Landscaping Checklist.* www.firewise.org/usa/files/fwlistsz.pdf. Accessed October 7, 2006.

Trapped Moisture

Joseph Lstiburek and John Carmody. *Moisture Control Handbook: Principles and Practices for Residential and Small Commercial Buildings.* John Wiley & Sons, 1994.

Lewis Harriman III, G.W. Brundrett and R. Kittler. *Humidity Control Design Guide: For Commercial and Institutional Buildings.* American Society of Heating, Refrigerating and Air Conditioning Engineers, 2001.

Joseph Lstiburek. *Builder's Guide: Cold Climates.* Energy Efficient Building Association and Shelter Source, 1997.

Joseph Lstiburek. *Builder's Guide: Mixed-Humid Climates.* Energy Efficient Building Association and Shelter Source, 1997.

Joseph Lstiburek. *Builder's Guide: Hot-Dry and Mixed-Dry Climates.* Energy Efficient Building Association and Shelter Source, 1997.

Joseph Lstiburek. *Builder's Guide: Hot-Humid Climates.* Energy Efficient Building Association and Shelter Source, 1997.

William B. Rose. *Water in Buildings: An Architect's Guide to Moisture and Mold.* John Wiley & Sons, 2005.

Foundations

Steven Winter. *The Rehab Guide: Foundations.* Prepared by Steven Winter Associates, Inc. for the US Department of Housing and Urban Development, Office of Policy Development and Research, Affordable Housing Research and Technology Division.

Walls

Steven Winter. *The Rehab Guide: Exterior Walls.* Prepared by Steven Winter Associates, Inc. for the US Department of Housing and Urban Development, Office of Policy Development and Research, Affordable Housing Research and Technology Division.

Financial Impacts

Institute for Business and Home Safety. *Fortified ... for safer living.* www.ibhs.org/property_protection/default.asp?id = 8. Accessed September 19, 2006.

Resources

East Coast Lightning Equipment, Inc.
24 Lanson Drive, Winsted, CT 06098
860-379-9072
Website: www.ecle.biz
Manufacturer of state-of-the-art lightning protection systems for structures of all types.

Gerard Roofing Technologies
955 Columbia Street, Brea, CA 92821
714-529-0407
Website: www.gerardusa.com
Stone Coated Steel Roofs with excellent resistance to fire, wind, hail, snow and ice. Their website has information about insurance discounts and energy rebates.

Hurricane Depot
10456 SW 184 Terrace, Miami, FL 33157
305-251-4283
Website: www.hurricanedepot.com
A wide variety of storm panels, garage braces and assorted hardware for hurricanes and other storms.

Lightning Rod Stuff
9401 N. 111th Drive, Sun City, AZ 85351
623-518-6170
Website: www.lightningrodstuff.com
Mail order supplier with an assortment of fancy ornamental and antique style lightning rods, weather vanes and accessories.

MinnSNOWta, Inc.
906 East White Street, Ely, MN 55731
218-365-6000
Website: www.minnsnowta.com
Roof rake snow removal system allows you to remove snow from the roof while standing on the ground.

Nelson Heat Tracing Systems
P. O. Box 726, Tulsa, OK 74101
918-627-5530
Website: www.nelsonheaters.com
Low energy-consumption electric roof and gutter de-icing system and a pipe warming system that automatically monitors temperatures and adjusts heat output as necessary to remain above freezing.

Professional Discount Supply(PDS)
19 W. Las Vegas Street, Colorado Springs, CO, 80903
800-688-5776; 719-444-0646
Website: www.radonpds.com
Mail order supplier of Radon mitigation supplies and test equipment.

Restoration Consultants, Inc.
3284 Ramos Circle, Sacramento, CA 95827
916-736-1100
Website: www.restcon.com
John Banta and a team of experts offer consultation services for disaster recovery, water damage, mold and other indoor air quality problems in homes and other buildings. Thermal imaging and a range of building diagnostic tools and equipment are available.

Simpson Strong-Tie Co. Inc
P.O. Box 10789, 5956 W. Las Positas Blvd., Pleasanton, CA 94588
(800) 999-5099
Website: www.strongtie.com
Leading manufacturer of structural connectors, anchors, fasteners and other construction aids for new construction, retrofitting and do-it-yourself.

Tornado Safe Room
P.O. Box 10238, Murfreesboro, TN 37129
877-723-7666
Website: www.tornadosaferoom.com
Custom-made and kit tornado safe rooms.

Index

Page numbers in italics indicate
photographs and diagrams.

About the Author

John C. Banta is certified by the American Board of Industrial Hygiene as a Certified Associate Industrial Hygienist with a Bachelors Degree in Environmental Health Science and 20 years of experience in Indoor Environmental Quality. He is a specialist in microbiological problems resulting from water damage in buildings. John is a Certified Mold Remediator, an Applied Microbial Remediation Technician and an approved instructor for both the Indoor Air Quality Association and Institute for Inspection, Cleaning and Restoration Certification and has taught classes throughout the US and Canada as well as in Australia and England. He has conducted investigations, trained technicians, established worker safety and health programs and supervised crews in sewage, flood, fungal remedia tion and disaster restoration throughout the United States. He is the co-author of the book titled Prescriptions for a Healthy House: A Practical Guide for Architects, Builders, and Homeowners.

If you have enjoyed *Extreme Weather Hits Home* you might also enjoy other

BOOKS TO BUILD A NEW SOCIETY

Our books provide positive solutions for people who want to make a difference. We specialize in:

**Environment and Justice • Conscientious Commerce
Sustainable Living • Ecological Design and Planning
Natural Building & Appropriate Technology • New Forestry
Educational and Parenting Resources • Nonviolence
Progressive Leadership • Resistance and Community**

New Society Publishers

ENVIRONMENTAL BENEFITS STATEMENT

New Society Publishers has chosen to produce this book on Enviro 100, recycled paper made with **100% post consumer waste**, processed chlorine free, and old growth free.

For every 5,000 books printed, New Society saves the following resources:[1]

35	Trees
3,160	Pounds of Solid Waste
3,477	Gallons of Water
4,536	Kilowatt Hours of Electricity
5,745	Pounds of Greenhouse Gases
25	Pounds of HAPs, VOCs, and AOX Combined
9	Cubic Yards of Landfill Space

[1]Environmental benefits are calculated based on research done by the Environmental Defense Fund and other members of the Paper Task Force who study the environmental impacts of the paper industry.

For a full list of NSP's titles, please call **1-800-567-6772** *or check out our website at:*

www.newsociety.com

NEW SOCIETY PUBLISHERS